# SECRETS OF THE
# MAZE

ADRIAN FISHER & HOWARD LOXTON

# SECRETS OF THE
# MAZE

ADRIAN FISHER & HOWARD LOXTON

**BARNES & NOBLE**
NEW YORK

©1997 Quarto Publishing plc

This 2007 edition published by
Barnes and Noble Inc.,
by arrangement with
Quantum Books Ltd

ISBN-13: 978-0-7607-9073-1
ISBN-10: 0-7607-9073-6

Printed in China by SNP Leefung

1 3 5 7 9 10 8 6 4 2

# CONTENTS

# INTRODUCTION

This book introduces you to the magic of the maze, explains some of its mysteries, and recounts some of its history. It also offers you a great many mazes to puzzle your way out of. Mazes are rooted in myth. They have existed for thousands of years in numerous forms all around the world. They have been used as a means of meditation and magic, adopted as ornamental garden features, and planned to provide lighthearted recreation. Today they are evolving in exciting new directions with innovative designs. But whether designed for entertainment, as art objects, or for contemplative purposes, mazes continue to offer both mystery and challenge to any who follow their paths. In these pages you can trace their development, experience for yourself their spiritual power, and test and develop your own skills as a maze-solver.

The English language has two words, labyrinth and maze, to denote a circuitous path that confuses the person following it. Here we mainly confine the term labyrinth to a unicursal, or single, path that has no junctions or choices, and use the words puzzle maze to describe a path that is broken to provide choices of route, some of which lead to dead-ends or into a deeper complexity of choices. For the rest, this book is plain-speaking. Maze designers may utilize mathematics and technology in creating mazes, but you need instinct rather than special skills to solve them. People with an especially good visual memory and sense of orientation may be at an advantage, but everyone will have fun.

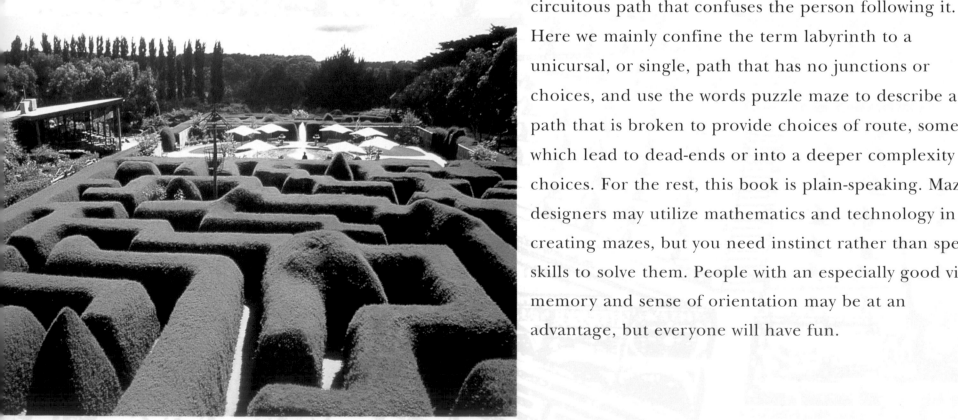

**BELOW**

*Ashcombe Maze at Shoreham in Victoria, Australia, is a modern example of the archetypal hedge maze.*

## SOLVING THE MAZES

When you take up the challenge to solve the maze puzzles in this book, you can use a transparent sheet of acetate, which can be bought very cheaply from stationers and craft stores. Place it over the plan of the maze that you want to solve, and draw on the sheet with a fine-tipped pen. You can then trace your route along the path of your choice without marking the book. When you have found the correct path and reached the goal, you can wipe the sheet clean and try another maze; you can also return to any maze and have an unmarked plan.

Don't take the easy way and travel the mazes with their entire plans laid out before you – although with some of the complex mazes, that would still present a challenge. Simulate the problems you would experience if walking through the real mazes. You could not see around corners or over hedges, or take in the entire pattern of a pavement maze. You can achieve this easily by cutting a small hole in a piece of card. Place the card on top of the maze you want to follow, ensuring the hole you have cut is positioned over the start of the maze, then move it along the path, so that as you choose your route, you genuinely make decisions without being able to see what is around the corner.

To increase the fun, especially in some of the simpler mazes, you are sometimes given additional problems to solve or trophies to collect. The rules are explained as you go, though if you wish, you can ignore them and trace an easier route.

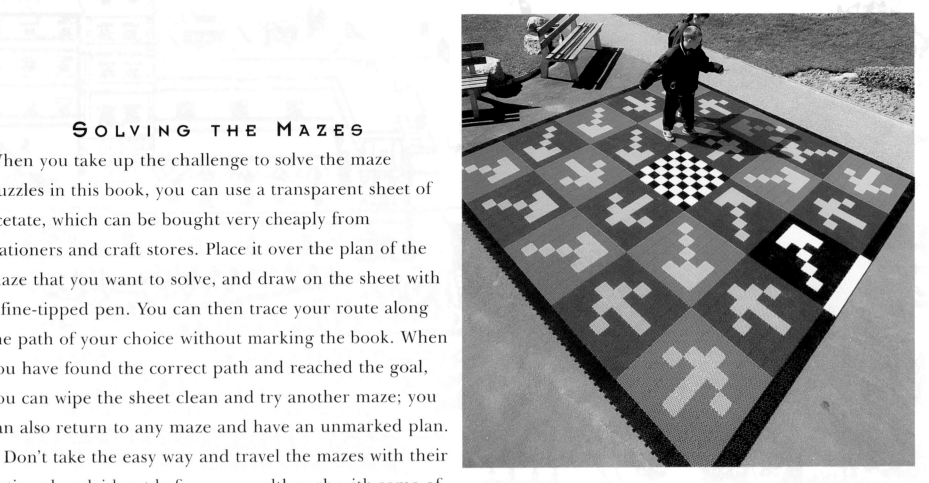

**ABOVE**

*This modern color maze, created by Adrian Fisher, is on a much smaller scale than most mazes you will find in the landscape but provides just as much fun.*

# ANCIENT LINKS

In Western cultures the idea of the maze is inextricably linked with the legend of the Greek hero Theseus. His mother, a princess of Troezen in the Peloponnesus, had been loved by both Aegeus, King of Athens, and the god Poseidon, so Theseus claimed both as his father. Raised at his mother's court, he journeyed as a young man to Athens, killing monsters and villains along the way, and asserted his right to Aegeus' throne.

The Athenians had been defeated in battle by King Minos of Crete, and in reparation for the death of his son, King Minos exacted from them the annual tribute of seven maidens and seven youths to be devoured by the monster known as the Minotaur. This creature, with a human body and the head of a bull, was the result of a union between Queen Pasiphaë and a great white bull sent to Crete by Poseidon. He had caused the queen to become infatuated with the bull after Minos had failed to offer it to him in sacrifice. Not daring to have the Minotaur killed, Minos ordered the inventor Daedalus to create a prison in which to contain the creature. This prison was known as the labyrinth, a place from which none could return unless they knew the secret of its tortuous passageways.

Theseus insisted on going to Crete as one of the tributes. At the court of Minos, the young Greeks were entertained as guests until the time came for them to be offered to the monster. Minos' daughter Ariadne was captivated by the Greek prince and fell in love with him. She revealed the secret of the labyrinth to Theseus, and gave him a ball of thread to unwind as he entered so that he could retrace his steps. Theseus killed the Minotaur, emerged from the

**ABOVE**
*This 18th-century etching shows the Minotaur in a walled labyrinth. The motto translates as "In silence and hope."*
**RIGHT**
*The turf maze at Saffron Walden in southern England is the largest surviving ancient turf labyrinth in Europe. Its design is similar to that found in many medieval churches.*

labyrinth, and immediately set sail for Athens with his fellow Greeks – and Ariadne.

They sailed first to the sacred island of Delos, where they celebrated their escape with dances, and then to Naxos, where Theseus abandoned Ariadne to the god Dionysus. As they approached Athens, Theseus failed to change the ship's black sails for white ones to signal his return alive. Believing Theseus dead, Aegeus flung himself from the clifftop to his death. Theseus thus became King of Athens. The Theseus story's contrasting elements of heroism, inventiveness, animalism, sexuality, devotion, treachery, revenge,

**PREVIOUS PAGE**
*The Sun and Moon Mazes in front of Longleat House in southern England make a stunning impact.*

# "THESEUS SLAYING THE MINOTAUR" PAVEMENT MAZE

This pavement maze was created as a permanent exhibit at Florida's Norton Museum of Art in the United States. It is made of 13,500 fired clay bricks laid in six colors. The central image of Theseus slaying the Minotaur is based on a Roman mosaic labyrinth at Cormerod in Switzerland. Enter the maze at the foot of the design, and travel along the gold and cream paths. The darker colors represent the barriers of the maze. Finally, enter the body of Theseus, and travel through his body and that of the Minotaur until you reach the Minotaur's head. As with the best Greek heroes, the weakest part of Theseus is his heel.

**ABOVE**

*The Theseus Slaying the Minotaur Maze was conceived as a representation of the triumph of freedom.*

and remorse have been variously emphasized and reinterpreted to suit the purposes of the teller for well over two thousand years. But is there any historical basis for the story of the labyrinth?

### FICTION OR FACT?

There was certainly a powerful and highly developed civilization in Crete, which had trade links with Egypt and other lands around the Mediterranean, and possessed either colonies or client states on the Greek mainland. It was swept away, probably as a consequence of the cataclysmic eruption of the volcano on the island that we now call Thera or Santorini, in about 1400 BC.

Bulls played a significant part in the religious and court life of this civilization, which came to be known as Minoan: in the large palace complex of Crete's ancient capital Knossos, the English archeologist Sir Arthur Evans (1851–1941) discovered bull's horns and bull figures, and murals that show dancers or athletes leaping and somersaulting over bulls. No evidence of a specific labyrinth structure was found. However, a stepped slab of stone was found in the courtyard of another Cretan palace at Phaestus, and an engraved seal that appears to show a bull attempting to climb over a similar obstacle. These have been interpreted as evidence that bull leaping took place in the colonnaded courtyards, which were surrounded like a modern bullring with a barrier over which the dancers could vault to safety. The Knossos palace consisted of numerous rooms, corridors, steps, and courtyards that would have been highly confusing to a stranger. Could these have given rise to the idea of a maze, and the bull leaping, which probably led to injuries and bloodshed, have fueled the idea of young people being thrown to the Minotaur?

The Roman writer Pliny speaks of an Egyptian labyrinth that was already 3,600 years old when he recorded it in the 1st century AD. According to Pliny, it had provided the

inspiration for Daedalus when he built the Cretan labyrinth. Excavations at Faiyûm in northern Egypt by Sir Flinders Petrie (1853–1942) suggest that this was a huge multistoried, multichambered religious and administrative center in which again it was easy to get lost, especially in darkness. The tomb of an Etruscan general and a columned building on the Greek island of Lemnos are also described by classical writers as labyrinths, but no relevant structures have been found, nor any evidence of labyrinths like those shown on later Cretan coins – except perhaps the circular foundations of a small temple at Epidaurus in Greece, which dates from around the 4th century BC.

Pre-Roman labyrinths that match our modern expectations are known from depictions on coins, a clay tablet from southern Greece, a pot from Syria, and a painted Etruscan pitcher. More intriguing are the symbols found

### TOP
*These rock carvings in Cornwall, England, are often claimed to be ancient, but were probably cut in the 17th century.*

### ABOVE
*Rock carvings at Val Camonica in northern Italy have been dated to around 1000–500 BC.*

### LEFT
*Many ancient Cretan coins bear the symbol of the labyrinth.*

# BATH FESTIVAL MAZE

Mazes were chosen as the theme of an international music festival held at Bath, England. The Bath Festival Maze has distinctive key-pattern turns and elliptical stone paths laid in grass. At the center is an Italian marble mosaic containing a river god's head, surrounded by six apses celebrating the four seasons, the four elements, and the Celtic and Roman history of the city.

This humorous interpretation of the Bath Maze offers a puzzling network of water pipes, allowing water to flow from the hot springs to the ancient Roman Baths. Find a way to let the hot water through, opening the fewest number of faucets. How many faucets do you need to turn? Remember, you can also wander the paths of the maze without trying to solve the extra puzzle we have added.

### RIGHT

*The mosaic at the center of the Bath Festival Maze contains "Gaze Mazes," which are solved visually.*

**ABOVE**

*This Etruscan terracotta wine jar, showing a labyrinth that appears to be labeled "Troy," dates back to the 7th century BC.*

carved into rocks in Sardinia (which may be 4000–4500 years old), in southern India, and in northern Italy. These are all variations of the same design: a seven-ringed unicursal labyrinth.

### ROMAN LABYRINTHS

Whatever its history, this design and derivations of it were well known in the Roman world. They appear as graffiti on the walls of the ancient ruins of Pompeii, and as patterns on the mosaic floors of Roman villas from Britain to eastern Europe and south to the colonies of North Africa. They are certainly linked with the Minotaur: his killing is sometimes featured in the mosaics; and a labyrinth scratched on a Pompeian wall bears the caption, "Here lives the Minotaur."

The labyrinth pattern most often found on Roman floors is not of concentric rings but a modification that more conveniently fits a rectangular room. It is composed of straight lines, usually turning at right angles. In its simplest form, the path traverses each quarter of the space in turn, each section being a reminder of the seven-ring pattern.

It is unlikely that the Romans performed any ritual walking through such mosaic labyrinths; they are too small in scale. Their purpose may have been symbolic: to protect against harm. Some incorporate details that suggest fortifications or a walled city. On the Etruscan

## SEVILLE ROMAN MOSAIC MAZE

This Roman mosaic labyrinth at Seville, Spain, has a mosaic pattern representing twisted rope, possibly alluding to the golden thread with which Theseus solved the archetypal Cretan labyrinth. Unusually, the Minotaur at the center is portrayed as a bull to his waist, unlike the more usual depiction of him with a bull's head. The entrance to the maze is the white path opposite the gate into this symbolic city. Your route around the maze will move first into the middle and then out again as you pass through each segment. The designs of almost all Roman mosaic mazes are variations on this form.

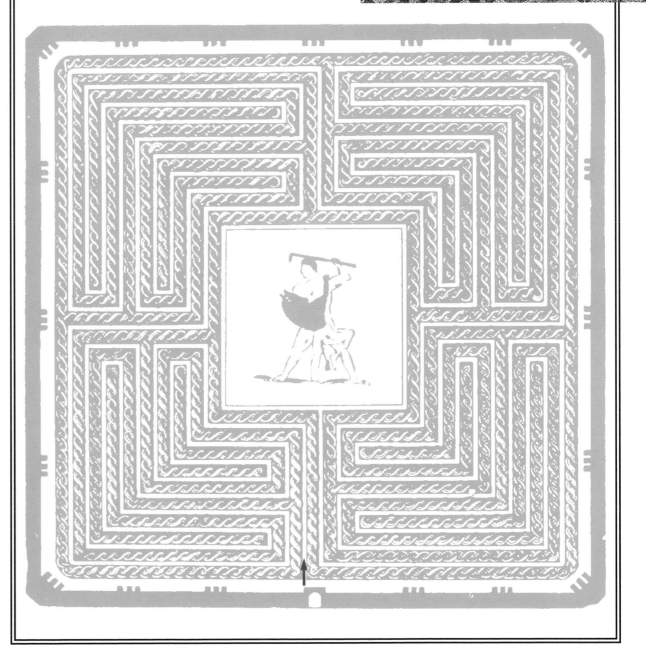

# LONGLEAT SUN MAZE

The Sun Maze at Longleat House in southern England is a symbolic maze. Within its design are images of the sun, the Minotaur, a maiden, a double-headed axe, and much more. The stylized head of the Minotaur in reverse becomes the head of Bacchus or Dionysus. Enter the maze from the left. The goal is the pool of water at the top of the design. Your path will take you in and out of the formal hedge maze along its gravel paths, around bushes, and across grass and lawns.

**ABOVE**
*An overview of the gravel Sun Maze at lake's edge, taken from the roof of Longleat House.*

pitcher, there are figures and an inscription that link the labyrinth with the city of Troy, birthplace of Aeneas, legendary forefather of the Romans, and perhaps also with a ceremony known as the *Ludus Troiae* (the "Game of Troy"). This was performed by groups of patrician Roman youths and consisted of circling maneuvers on horseback, which were labyrinthine in nature. In medieval manuscripts, a labyrinth is often used to symbolize a city, and this may have been inherited from the Romans. However, parallels can also be found in Indian culture, where labyrinthine defenses possess magic power. In actual fortifications, an approach through labyrinthine walls not only confuses potential invaders but makes them vulnerable to attack from the defenders.

### AMERICAN LABYRINTHS

North America also has rock carvings of labyrinths, although it is difficult to prove a date for them. Were they indigenous, or was the design derived from Europe? A pattern scratched into the adobe wall of a building at Casa Grande in Arizona has been offered as evidence that the design was known before contact with Europeans, because the site was abandoned long before Europeans arrived there.

A labyrinth features in a myth of the Native American Pima, which tells of Iitoi (the "Elder Brother"), a good man saved, like Noah, when flood destroyed an evil world. Iitoi helped to create the ancestors of the Pima and of the Tohono O'otam people, and taught them skills. Men of later times turned against him and killed him, but his spirit returned and evaded capture by taking a maze of paths where none could follow. Iitoi and his labyrinth are still depicted in the Native American craftwork design known as the House of Iitoi, which can also be seen as a symbol of the twists and turns of life.

In South America, a labyrinth shape occurs among the huge, mysterious markings on the plains northwest of Nazca, Peru. The "Nazca lines" have been dated to between the 5th and 13th centuries AD. Although this is a very broad dating, they are certainly pre-Columbian in origin, which again provides evidence that their design did not originate in Europe. Perhaps the circling pattern of the classical labyrinth, with its alternate sweeps from side to side, reaches deep into the human psyche and developed separately in many different cultures.

**ABOVE**
*This stone labyrinth is laid out on the rocks above an old seasonal fishing harbor in Sweden.*

**BELOW RIGHT**
*The labyrinth design is often featured in Native American Hopi and Pima craftwork and jewelry.*

### STONE LABYRINTHS AND THEIR RITUALS

The classical labyrinth pattern seen on Cretan coins is found in Scandinavia, marked out by large stones. There are over 600 examples of this kind, some many centuries old, and their distribution ranges from Iceland to Russia. Even in Denmark, where no old labyrinths survive, there are many place names, such as Trojborg, which indicate a former site – and the tradition of building labyrinths continues.

The name Trojborg ("Troy town"), a link with the legendary Greek heroes and with the Roman labyrinths, is sometimes applied to a labyrinth itself. Others are known by titles such as Jerusalem, Jericho, or Nineveh. They may simply have been named for a famous and religiously

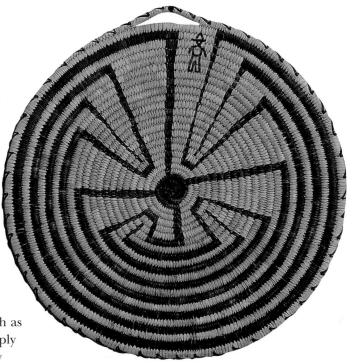

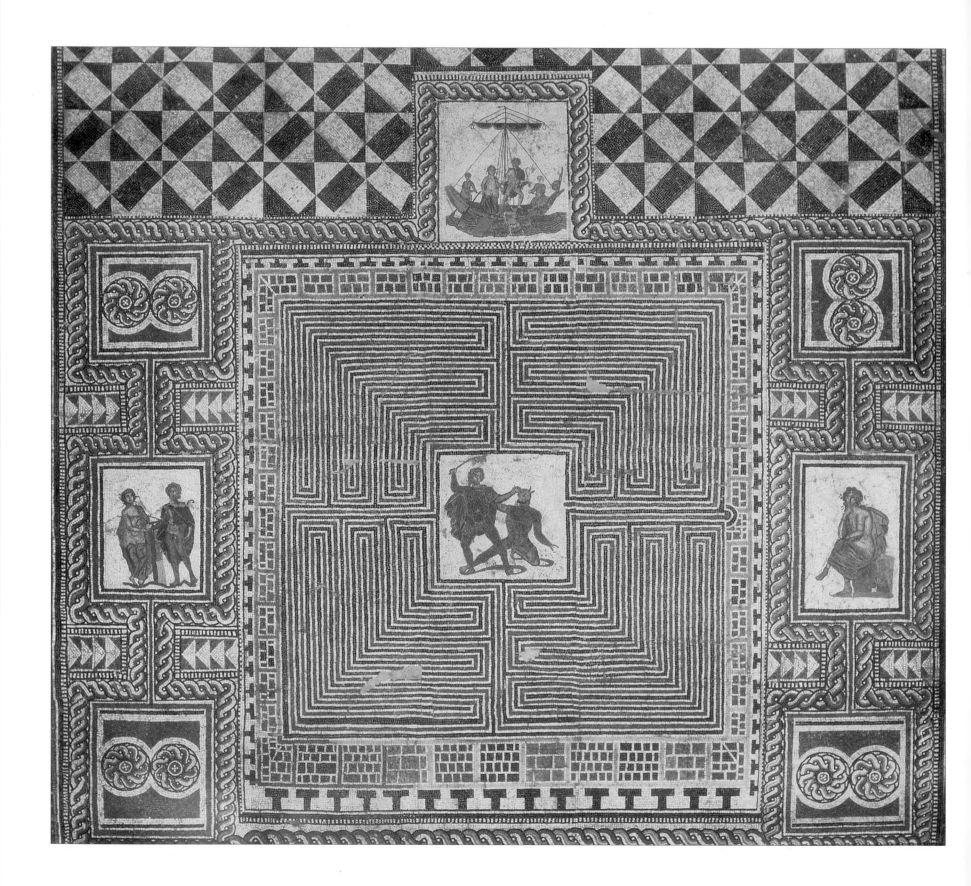

## SALZBURG ROMAN MOSAIC MAZE

This Roman mosaic labyrinth found near Salzburg in Austria contains cameos illustrating aspects of the story of Theseus and the Minotaur. Its four quarters of pathways are identical, each rotated a further 90 degrees clockwise. Again, the labyrinth is surrounded by a city wall with battlements, and just one entrance gate. The twisted rope motif, popular in Roman times, is extensively used in the design.

There is clearly just a single path to follow. As an extra challenge, try to estimate the total path length involved. The entire mosaic area measures 21 x 18 feet (6 x 5.5 m).

important city, but there is an intriguing parallel between the rings of the labyrinth and the Bible story of the Israelites circling the walls of Jericho. Was this a memory of the city's labyrinthine fortifications – though there is no archeological evidence that the ancient Canaanite city possessed such protection?

Many Scandinavian labyrinths were constructed on the shores of the Baltic Sea. Today sea level is considerably lower than it was a few centuries ago. The labyrinths close to the shore would not have been built when their sites were underwater, so an

earliest date can be established for them. This, and a dating technique based on a study of lichen growth since the stones were placed, indicates that most do not predate the 13th or 14th century, and many are much more recent. Away from the coast or on high ground, especially where labyrinths are found near burial sites and other evidence of ancient occupation, earlier dates can be more reliably established. Some go back to the Iron Age (though this came to the north considerably later than in the Mediterranean lands, in about 1000 BC).

## THE CLASSICAL SEVEN-RING LABYRINTH

There are three main forms of unicursal labyrinth: Classical, Roman, and medieval Christian. All three forms share a hidden characteristic: internal rotational symmetry. The archetypal unicursal labyrinth is the Classical seven-ring design.

Step 1: Draw a cross and four points at each corner in a square design.
Step 2: Join the top arm of the cross to the top left point.
Step 3: Join the right arm of the cross to the top right point.
Step 4: Join the left arm of the cross to the bottom left point.
Step 5: Join the bottom arm of the cross to the bottom right point.

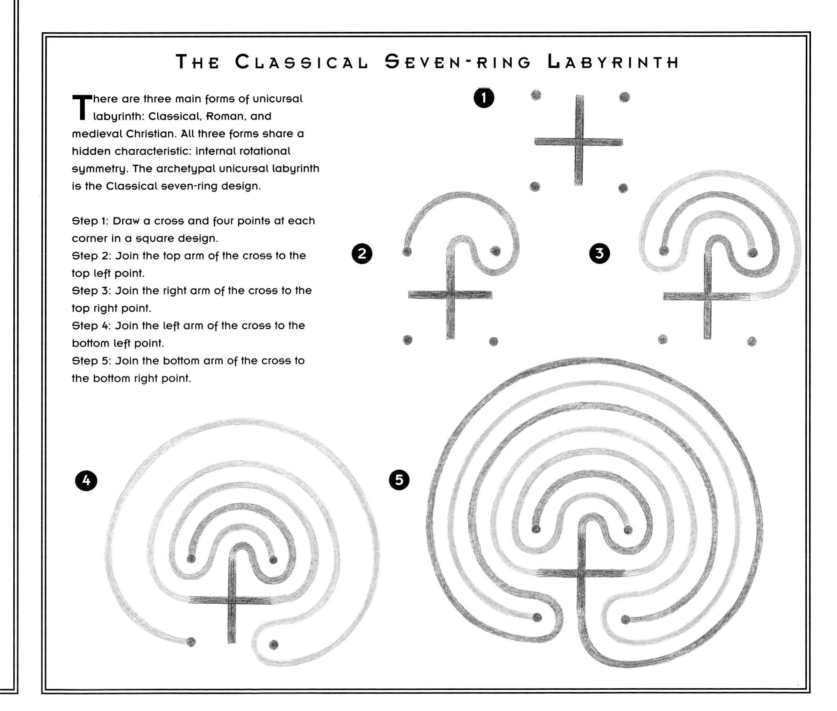

**LEFT**
*This maze on the island of St. Agnes, one of the Scilly Isles, was photographed in 1885 with the wreck of the Earl of Lonsdale in the background. Known as "Troy Town," tradition states that the maze was laid out in 1729, but its design has been modified in later restorations.*

**BELOW**
*This pictorial representation of the Minotaur, from the center of the Bath Festival Maze, was designed as a "Gaze Maze." Trace a path from one horn to the other with your eyes, always keeping to the white mosaic pieces.*

The early inland labyrinths are often placed on the line of eskers, ridged deposits left by retreating glaciers, which provided abundant suitable stones. They are scattered many miles apart, but each was probably sited close enough to the nearest ancient settlement for the local population to gather there in less than a day's journeying. Their function was surely ceremonial, possibly religious. The coastal labyrinths, on the other hand, are often found in clusters. Most of them were probably constructed after the Christianization of the area, but surviving traditions and old tales indicate their use in fertility rites, or at least mating games. For example, a young woman would stand within the labyrinth, and others would dance in to join her; some labyrinths in Finland are even known as "virgin dances." In Sweden, a labyrinth named "the Virgin Ring" has two entrances, through which a pair of youths raced to be first to reach a waiting girl.

Such rites echo ancient beliefs and ceremonies connected with the release of a goddess from the underworld of winter to bring fertility. Other stories make the labyrinths the homes of trolls from whom a stolen girl had to be freed. On the coast, where they are sometimes close to navigational markers, building a labyrinth was thought to secure more favorable sailing weather.

# ROBIN HOOD'S RACE

This variation of the medieval Christian labyrinth design is a plan of the maze known as Robin Hood's Race at Sneinton, near Nottingham, England, which was ploughed up in 1797. Several ancient turf labyrinths were named after the popular hero Robin Hood, alluding perhaps to his reputation for rushing into Sherwood Forest and thus evading capture by the Sheriff of Nottingham. Sadly, none of the turf mazes bearing his name has survived.

There are no junctions or choices to be made, yet you will find that the twists and turns of the single path are remarkably compelling to follow, whether walking, running, or on paper. The plan of this maze also bears similarities to that in Chartres Cathedral, France (see page 32), though with the addition of bastions. It is thought that at some time it was miscut, creating this irregular pattern. Can you see where the errors might have occurred?

## TURF LABYRINTHS

Labyrinths also exist on the other side of the Baltic Sea, in Germany and Poland. A German labyrinth in Steigra is known as the "Swede's Ring," and another in Greitchen as "Swede's Cut." This gave rise to a theory that the labyrinth concept passed south from Scandinavia rather than north from the Mediterranean, but there is no real evidence to support it. The German labyrinths are not marked out with stones, but are cut in turf. Only four old examples are known to have survived, though there are more modern versions. All the original labyrinths are rounded in form. Those in Steigra and Greitchen are eleven-ring labyrinths. The Rad (Wheel), in the Eilcnrcidc Forest near Hanover, has nine rings. In the part of Pomerania now in Poland, there was a nineteen-ring labyrinth at Stolp variously known as "Winding Path" or "City of Winding." The present labyrinth at Stolp dates from only 1935, but replaces an earlier one which was, until 1909, the scene of a festival held by the Guild of Shoemakers once every three years, during which songs and dances were performed in its circles.

## OLD ENGLISH TURF MAZES

Turf mazes once existed in Denmark, but none survive today. In Britain, however, there are extant turf mazes, and the evidence of place names suggests that they were once numerous.

Sometimes their path is a channel cut into the turf; sometimes the channel forms the barrier between grass paths. The English patterns vary considerably: those at Somerton in Oxfordshire and Dalby in Yorkshire resemble the Scandinavian or Cretan labyrinths; others are adaptations of Roman mosaic designs; and some are entirely individual. Seven ancient English turf mazes survive, sixty additional sites have been identified, and it seems likely that at least another hundred have disappeared. It is not known how old the existing mazes are. Even if one were excavated, regular restoration over the centuries, which would tend to remove earth rather than add layers, might have destroyed valuable evidence. Maze names again include "Troy Town" or "Walls of Troy," "Julian's Bower" (which some historians have attempted to link, via Julius Caesar, with the *Ludus Troiae*), and the more everyday "Mazle" and "Mizmaze." The Welsh name is *Caerdroia*, which can be translated either as "City of Troy," or, if read as *caer y troiae*, as the "City of Turnings."

There is a tradition that the maze in Sneinton, near Nottingham, was made by priests from the nearby Chapel of St. Anne (built in 1490), as a place for them to exercise. Known as "Robin Hood's Race" or "Shepherd's Race," it was certainly raced in by children. However, the tradition of its origin seems to have been started by a 19th-century historian. At Alkborough in Humberside, local belief has it that their maze was built as a penance by one of the knights who murdered St. Thomas Becket in Canterbury Cathedral in 1170, but again there is no evidence.

# JULIAN'S BOWER

This turf maze at Alkborough, England, is popularly known as Julian's Bower and is considered to date back to the early 13th century. A traditional story connected with the maze tells of a river spirit known as Gur, who took exception to the cutting of the maze on the hillside above his river and the visiting Christian pilgrims. To frighten the visitors to Jerusalem (as this maze was also called locally), he sent a great wave up the river in an attempt to wash the maze and the pilgrims away, but the effort was in vain, for the wave was not high enough to do any damage. He continues to try with each spring tide, when the Trent Bore (a small tidal wave) races up the river past Alkborough.

LEFT

*The Alkborough turf maze is sunk in a deep hollow, which suggests many centuries of renovation when the gulleys between the pathways have been cleared.*

In both Britain and Germany, firm documentation is generally of a much later date. The former "Magic Circle" in Eberswalde, Germany, was cut by a schoolmaster in 1609 for his pupils to play in; the Hilton maze in Cambridgeshire, England, has a stone pillar that records its cutting in 1660. However, such records may be evidence not of first construction but of renovation. We know from contemporary sources, including William Shakespeare, that mazes were an established part of popular culture in Elizabethan England, so we can reasonably assume that they had been around for some time.

Mazes were disapproved of by the Puritans. The 1660 date in Hilton is that of the restoration of

**LEFT**
*This plan of the labyrinth at Rippon Common in northern England is another typical example of a turf maze. You can easily see the resemblances between this maze and Julian's Bower on the previous page.*

## VERONICA'S MAZE

**T**his maze at Parham Park in southern England is one of the most delightful examples of a maze where a hard path, in this case made of brick, is laid in grass. The effect is of walking around a verdant lawn, while remaining on a dry, firm path. It is deceptively simple compared to many modern mazes, but is in fact a modern maze with junctions. The flat path in the grass and its apparent simplicity echo ancient turf mazes, giving it an historic ambience. Once you start, you must keep going forward. When you reach forks in the path, you choose which way to go. You must not double back when joined by other paths, nor make right-angled turns where paths cross over each other.

**LEFT**
*Veronica's Maze was inspired by one of the embroidery bed coverlets from the house that is situated in the grounds of the park.*

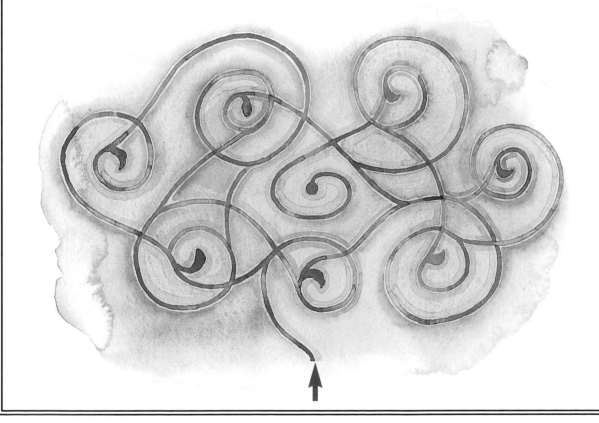

RIGHT

**RIGHT**

*The Braemore Mizmaze in Hampshire, England, is dramatically located in the middle of lush woodlands.*

**BELOW**

*Documentary evidence records that the turf maze at Hilton was either created or recut in 1660, at the time of the restoration of Charles II to the British throne.*

King Charles II after the fall of Cromwell's Puritan commonwealth, so it may have been recut in celebration of a return to old ways. It is not surprising that there is no sign of turf mazes being made by the early settlers in the North American colonies: even if the rigors of the pioneering life had allowed time for such activities, they would not have been considered suitable diversions. Mazes were considered frivolous, but there is no record of their being criticized as papist. In fact, there is no evidence of English mazes being used in Christian ritual. The similarity of those in Braemore, Hilton, Saffron Walden, and Winchester to the pavement design found in some medieval French churches does suggest a connection, although such pavements are unknown in England. It is possible that they predate the Middle Ages, and their designs were modified to create the Christian images.

# SAFFRON WALDEN TURF MAZE

**E**urope's largest surviving ancient turf maze lies on the Common at Saffron Walden in Essex, England, with a path of nearly one mile. Its sculptured earthworks and corner bastions give it a distinctive character. A record of the costs of recutting in 1699 survives, but it is probably much older. An 18th-century document records: "The Maze at Saffron Walden is the gathering place of the young men of the district who have a system of rules connected with walking the maze, and wagers in gallons of beer are frequently won or lost. For a time it was used by the beaux and belles of the town, a young maiden standing in the center, known as home, while the boy tried to get to her in record time without stumbling."

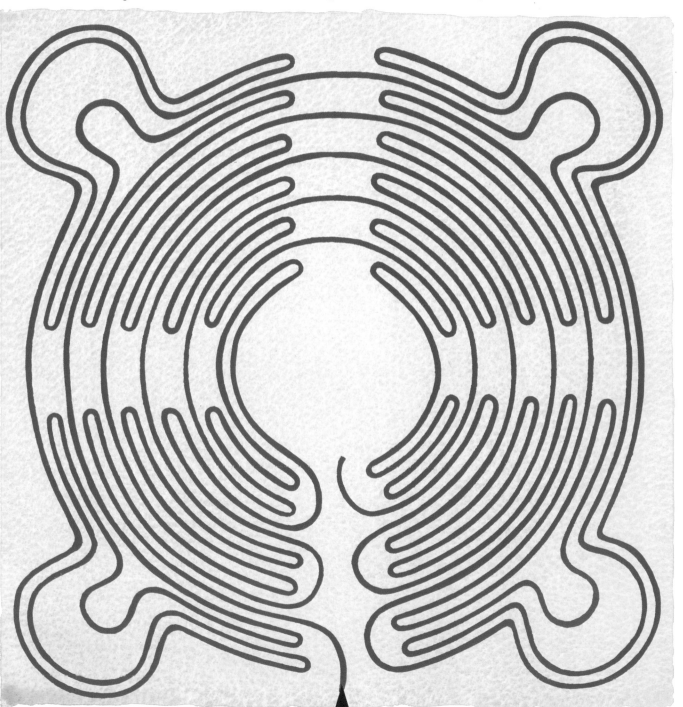

**BELOW**
*This detail of the turf maze at Saffron Walden shows one of the four distinctive bastions.*

# PIMPERNE TURF MAZE

English labyrinth use, as in Scandinavia and Germany, suggests a connection with fertility rites. Folk culture made seasonal festivities of many ceremonies that were once pagan rituals: the May Day dances around the maypole, for example, with their circling patterns have similarities to labyrinth paths. Intriguingly, the turf maze known as the Shepherd's Ring or Shepherd's Race in Boughton Green, Northampton, which survived until World War I, was associated, like the one at Stolp, with a local Guild of Shoemakers. The names of such labyrinths alone are evidence that races were held in them. In Dalby, the path is

**ABOVE**

*The design of this English turf maze, formerly at Boughton Green, intriguingly ends in a spiral.*

banked to help runners take the turns at speed. In Wing, in Leicestershire, there used to be a raised bank beside the maze to provide spectators with a better view of the runners. The name Wing comes from the Norse Vengi; Dalby is in an area colonized by the Danes; and the presence of mazes in parts of England that were settled by the Danes has been taken as evidence that they were introduced from Scandinavia. But there are also mazes in areas beyond the Danish influence. The siting of mazes in places where there are ancient earthworks (the Wing bank was probably an early tumulus, or burial mound) is cited to support the theory that the mazes are themselves ancient. Since neither argument can be proven, the mazes retain the secret of their origins.

The design of this turf maze is completely different from any other. Instead of closely packed concentric rings of paths, the path proceeds in irregular meanders. This plan seems to indicate the paths running in gullies rather than as raised strips of turf. In 1686 the antiquarian John Aubrey described it as "much used by the young people on Holydaies and by ye Schoolboies."

Sadly, this maze, at Pimperne in southern England, was ploughed up in 1730. However, John Bastard's meticulous drawing of 1758 still survives. Although it looks like a modern puzzle maze, its pattern in unicursal. Try to guess the order in which the four spaces within the design will be reached.

# WINCHESTER MIZMAZE

This turf maze lies on St. Catherine's Hill overlooking Winchester, the ancient capital of England. The name Mizmaze is particular to southern England, with the only other surviving example at Braemore. The Winchester Mizmaze is unusual in having the path in the gully, running between raised strips of grass. As a result, it has worn over the centuries to form a very pleasing series of rounded curves where the paths double back. The path itself poses no problems, but the way in which it curves when doubling back on itself is delightful.

### ABOVE

*By tradition, the maze at Winchester is supposed to have been made by a schoolboy who was kept behind during vacation for bad behavior.*

# One Way In

The Fathers of the Christian Church often countered the influence of pagan beliefs by taking over their symbols and ceremonies and giving them a significance appropriate to the Christian faith. Christmas, for example, replaced the pagan midwinter festival, Easter the celebration of spring. Labyrinths – and even the Minotaur – were given a place within the Church.

### EARLY CHURCH LABYRINTHS

The earliest known example of a labyrinth in a church is at El Asnam in Algeria. In Roman times, this was the town of Castellum Tingitanum, and here, in the 4th century, a mosaic pavement was laid in the Church of Reparatus which presents a typical Roman labyrinth pattern. In the center, however, replacing an image such as Theseus and the Minotaur, are rows of letters of the Latin alphabet. At first they appear meaningless, but if you identify the letter at the very center and read outward from it, up, down, or sideways – moving straight or at right angles and never along diagonals – any route you take will spell out *SANCTA ECCLESIA* ("HOLY CHURCH").

The choice of a labyrinth design, here and in Roman houses, may have no symbolic significance; it could simply have been a regular pattern that the craftsman knew. But the addition of a puzzle, and its location at the goal, suggest the believer's search for the truth of the faith and the protection of the Church.

The Church of San Vitale in Ravenna, Italy, which was built in the 6th century, has a circular labyrinth in the pavement in front of the high altar. It is in Byzantine style, and if it is contemporary with the church, it would be the

**ABOVE**
*The design of the Alkborough turf maze is reproduced on a tombstone in the local churchyard.*
**RIGHT**
*The Creation Maze at Värmlands Säby in Sweden is planted in the shape of a falcon's egg.*

next oldest surviving church labyrinth. However, flooding at the end of the 16th century made it necessary to relay part of the floor, so we cannot be certain. There may have been labyrinths in other early Christian churches. They certainly existed in some Italian churches of the early

**PREVIOUS PAGE**
*The hedge maze at Egeskov on Fyn Island, Denmark, dates from the 17th century.*

# CHARTRES CATHEDERAL PAVEMENT MAZE

The circular architectural form has long been associated with the churches of the Knights Templar. Traditionally, Christian churches faced east, pointing toward the Holy Land. However, when the Knights Templar reached the Holy Land during their Crusades, they began to build circular churches, like those they found in Jerusalem. It may well be that the Knights Templar were responsible for creating the famous circular labyrinth in Chartres Cathedral, France.

The Chartres labyrinth has often been used as a meditational fingermaze. Clear your mind and trace the path with your index finger. The path represents the journey through life from birth to salvation with all its circular meanders.

**LEFT**
*The Chartres labyrinth lies
beneath the great circular rose window,
whose size and shape it echoes. The plan appeared in a
17th-century sketchbook surrounded by this array of creatures.*

Middle Ages: those in Pavia, Piacenze, and two in Rome survive, together with one carved on a cathedral wall at Lucca.

### French Church Labyrinths

From the 12th century, labyrinths are found in some French churches also: as treadable pavement designs, in diminutive versions on decorative tiles, and carved on a wall. Five medieval French examples survive, and others are known to have existed. In the 16th century, a labyrinth was laid at the entrance to a chapel in Ghent, Belgium, and at least one existed in Germany, at Cologne. All are unicursal; most follow a similar design in curved or angular form, the path intermittently doubling within one quadrant then sweeping through two. The labyrinth in 13th-century Chartres Cathedral, near Paris, is usually regarded as the basic form, though it was not necessarily the first of its kind. At St. Omer in northern France, a design with a totally different appearance, which was also copied elsewhere, was nevertheless unicursal.

### Right

*This fountain in Damascus, Syria, channels its spring of water through a unicursal labyrinthine path.*

### St. Omer Pavement Maze

A pavement labyrinth was laid in the church of St. Omer in northern France in the 14th century, but destroyed in the 18th century. The original St. Omer labyrinth had a strong black and white form and a unicursal design. Here, new gaps through the barriers have been created to transform the unicursal labyrinth into a puzzle maze with junctions. Rectangles of primary colors have also been added to make the maze even more puzzling to solve. Your task is to trace a path through to the central goal. However, you must pass through each area of color in the following repeated sequence: Red–Blue–Yellow, Red-Blue-Yellow, etc.

# St. Quentin Pavement Maze

This striking octagonal labyrinth has the same pattern of turns as the labyrinth in Chartres Cathedral, yet here the paths are entirely formed of straight lines. If you look carefully at the design, you may be able to make out the distinctive shape of the Maltese Cross. It is thought that the maze may have been created by the Knights of St. John, with whom this symbol is associated, upon their return home to France from the Crusades. Follow the dark stones that form the path to the center of the maze.

LEFT
*Despite its angular form, the path of the St. Quentin maze follows the same turns as that of the Chartres maze.*

It is often stated that these church labyrinths were used for doing penance and as a substitute for pilgrimages to distant places, especially for those too infirm or otherwise unable to travel. The name *Chemin de Jérusalem* applied to some labyrinths, and *ciel* (heaven) or *Jérusalem* as their central goal seems to lend credence to this idea. However, the notion was not proposed until the 19th century, and there is no medieval evidence that traversing the labyrinth, whether on foot or on the knees, ever earned an indulgence to act in place of a pilgrimage; nor does the name *Chemin de Jérusalem* appear prior to the Renaissance. That does not mean, of course, that individuals could not undertake it as a self-appointed penance.

### Labyrinth Dances

What is certain is that some French church labyrinths were used for rituals that included choral dancing. A ceremony held at Auxerre in France on Easter Monday included the throwing of a ball between the dean, who led the singing, and his canons. There is a similarity to the ancient circle dance known as the carol – precursor of our modern Christmas carols. There may be a continuity here from some pagan original, but the celebration is an entirely Christian one, and its circular pattern seems likely to have echoed Christ's death and resurrection, and the medieval belief in the harrowing of hell, when Christ entered hell on one day a year to save lost souls.

The figures of Theseus and the Minotaur are found in connection with some church labyrinths. The legendary hero, who was thought to have a heavenly father in addition to his earthly one, becomes a forerunner of Christ, or represents Christ himself, entering hell to confront and vanquish the figure of evil. It should be remembered that Theseus was also said to have visited the Underworld, where in some versions of Greek mythology, Minos himself reigned as king following his earthly rule at Knossos. At Lucca Cathedral in Italy, an inscription by the labyrinth reminds the faithful that no one could leave the labyrinth except Theseus with Ariadne's aid: Ariadne perhaps representing the mediation and

## Segala's Ship

**F**rancesco Segala was a 15th-century Italian architect from Padua who created puzzle maze designs, mainly in figurative forms. His designs included ships, dolphins, crabs, dogs, snails, horsemen, and human figures. It is doubtful if any of his designs were actually constructed in hedges. If built full-size, some of them would have measured many hundreds of feet in length, covering up to five or six acres, which would have been prohibitively expensive. If such a maze had been made, it would certainly have appeared in contemporary engravings of major historic landscapes. The entrance to the maze is at the base of the design. Unbroken lines form the barriers to the maze and your goal is the crow's nest at the top of the central mast of the ship.

# ELY CATHEDERAL
# PAVEMENT MAZE

**T**he maze inside Ely Cathedral in southern England was created in 1870 during restoration work. Its total path length precisely matches the height of the West Tower, beneath which the pavement maze is laid. The entrance to this unicursal labyrinth is on the left, and the goal is at the center.

**ABOVE**
*The Ely maze is the only one to be found inside an English cathedral. It is unrelated to earlier Christian designs.*

teaching of the Church or the Virgin Mary.

There are possible echoes of the Theseus legend also in the dancing that took place in church labyrinths. On Delos, where Theseus danced his freedom with his fellow Greek youths and maidens, people used to perform the crane dance, which apparently imitated the courtship behavior of that bird but was described as circling in a pattern that closely resembled the classical labyrinth shape. It is also possible, however, that the pagan traditions of the north fed into ceremonies such as those in Auxerre.

By the end of the 12th century opposition had begun to the increasing dramatization of Easter rituals and to the labyrinth dances. The absence of pavement labyrinths in Britain may be due to the fact that turf mazes were widely used at local festivals and labyrinths were therefore considered too secular for churches, although there are some labyrinth carvings, such as those on roof bosses (ornamental projections) in Bristol and at South Tawton in Devon, in locations that could not be danced upon. Labyrinth ceremonies fell into disuse or were suppressed, though some perhaps still used them. Children played on church labyrinths, and it was the distraction of their games during services that led to the removal of the labyrinth in Reims, northeastern France, in the 18th century. However, the interest of the 19th century in all things gothic saw a reintroduction of labyrinths: first, a model based on the Chartres labyrinth, in Itchen Stoke in Hampshire, England, in about 1866; then a new design by Sir Gilbert Scott in Ely Cathedral, Cambridgeshire. Others followed in both England and France, and in Amiens, northern France, the labyrinth ripped out in the 1820s was later restored in 1894.

Today, most Christians regard the labyrinth as a metaphor for human life: a twisting path which brings sudden changes, temptations, and dangers, but which, if carefully negotiated in accordance with religious principles, will bring the soul safe to paradise. It is a metaphor which would have been equally appreciated in the Middle Ages.

### SPIRITUAL CENTERS
In 1991 Dr. Lauren Artress, Canon for Special Ministries at San Francisco's Grace Cathedral, walked a labyrinth for the first time, in a seminar run by a psychologist. This initial experience filled her with anxiety, but on a second occasion, she

"felt joyous one minute, burdened the next," and "[seemed] to step beyond time to where each moment stood triumphant in its own right." She became convinced that the labyrinth could be a valuable spiritual tool, and was instrumental in having a copy of the Chartres labyrinth painted on canvas and installed in Grace Cathedral, where it was used by groups and individuals in their efforts to be in touch with themselves and with God. A tapestry labyrinth has now replaced it, and a pavement labyrinth was laid outside. Dr. Artress has taken the canvas version to other locations, including prisons, and Grace Cathedral has founded an organization named Viriditas to encourage the use of labyrinths worldwide.

This was not the first modern American labyrinth, only the first ecclesiastical one. Alternative groups and New Age thinkers in the United States had been working with labyrinths since 1986, and in Europe they were a feature of such movements earlier still. Projekt Labyrinth was established in Zurich, Switzerland, in the mid-1980s by supporters of the Swiss and German women's movements. It promotes the use of labyrinths as centers for discussion and recreation as well as meditation. It inaugurated its own first

labyrinth in 1991. The form of its outdoor labyrinths shows the influence of the ancient stone and turf labyrinths of northern Europe, and they are often planted as gardens.

## GARDEN MAZES

The Romans trimmed hedges and shrubs in topiary shapes, but do not appear to have planted them as mazes. The first mentions of what were probably garden mazes or labyrinths appear in the 12th century as *dédales* or *maisons de dédale* (a reference to Daedalus), but it is not clear what form these took. One French source describes what sounds like a garden building, and another, detailing a garden inspired from Arab lands by a returning crusader, refers to a structure that may have been of trelliswork. It is not until the mid-15th century that a labyrinth can be identified as specifically of hedgework.

There are no clear descriptions or illustrations of these early garden mazes. Illuminations in medieval manuscripts use the maze symbolically or to accompany the Theseus story. Fifteenth-century Italian drawings and paintings of the Cretan labyrinth show high walls that emphasize its prison function. This could be the sort of

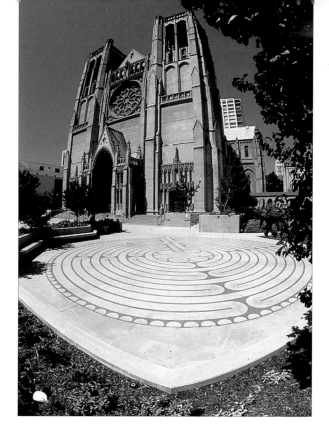

**ABOVE**
*The pavement maze in front of Grace Cathederal, San Francisco, is directly inspired by that at Chartres.*
**BELOW**
*A 15th-century Florentine painting, showing the Minotaur.*

# "THE DREAM OF POLIPHILO" HEDGE MAZE

**T**his giant hedge maze at the Château de Thoiry in France was inspired by Francesco Colonna's 15th-century book The Dream of Poliphilo, in which an elaborate water labyrinth is described. The dream was an allegory about the nature of architecture, and was a seminal work that helped bring about the Renaissance in Italian architecture. In the dream, Poliphilo enters the Dark Forest in search of his true love, Polia. She is finally to be found behind one of three doors, which symbolize Science, Art, and Love. The message is that true love, not mere calculation or aesthetics, should be the finest guide in all things.

The maze is in the shape of a giant eye, with a five-pointed star representing the five senses, together with the elephants and obelisks found in the original story, and an owl, fish, dove, and lizard representing the family of the owner of the maze. Enter the paths of the maze at the bottom edge of the design, and trace a route to the central red circle, which represents the Temple of Venus. There are nine bridges in the maze, which take the paths over and under each other. The two large arrows at the sides of the design represent two quick exits from the maze.

# THE SYMMETRY OF LABYRINTH DESIGN

At first glance, labyrinths can appear very complicated, with paths that weave around each other seemingly at random; their internal symmetry is not always apparent. However, this hidden symmetry can be demonstrated in all three forms of unicursal labyrinth: Classical (below), medieval Christian (right), and Roman (bottom).

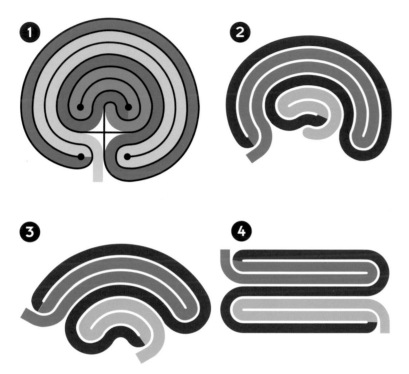

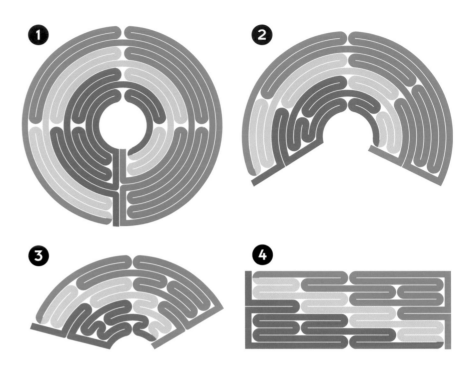

## CLASSICAL LABYRINTH
Make a vertical cut from the entrance of the design to its goal (1). Gradually fold the design out to form a rectangle (2 and 3), where its symmetry becomes obvious (4).

## MEDIEVAL CHRISTIAN LABYRINTH
Flatten out the design in the same way as the Classical labyrinth (1, 2, and 3). Again, it becomes obvious that the design is symmetrical, though this time the path sweeps exuberantly right around the design (4).

## ROMAN LABYRINTH
Note the labyrinth's four quadrants (1). Separate out each quarter of the design, and place them side by side (2). It is then easy to see that the same pattern is repeated in each quarter. Note also that each quarter resembles the flattened out Classical labyrinth (3).

structure that the Italian writer Boccaccio mentioned a century earlier in a commentary on Dante Alighieri's *Divine Comedy*. An English poem from the middle of the 15th century describes ladies in a labyrinth, confused by its turnings, and some of them stepping over its partitions to escape. Perhaps these were low fences, like those that later surrounded plots in Tudor gardens; or perhaps they were low hedges of the kind that became popular in the Elizabethan knot garden.

### NOBLE MAZES

An allegorical book titled *The Dream of Poliphilo*, written in 1467 by Francesco Colonna, an Italian monk, is partly set in a series of gardens, and takes the reader by boat through a water labyrinth. Its descriptions both reflected and influenced many Renaissance gardens. Although no water labyrinth is known to have been made, the suitability of a maze or labyrinth for a nobleman's garden was recognized, and some Italian gardens, such as that of Cardinal Gonzaga on the Quirinale in Rome, already possessed one. In the 16th century mazes became an established feature of the gardens of the European nobility, and of some lesser gardens also. No less than four were planned for the d'Este villa in Tivoli, near Rome. England's King Henry VIII had one at his Palace of Nonesuch, south of London; King Francis I of France had one in his garden at Cognac; the Emperor Charles V had labyrinths built in his Brussels garden, and at the Alcazar palace in Seville, Spain. Writers on gardening in France, the Netherlands, England, and Italy began to include designs for mazes in their books.

### ORNAMENTAL MAZES

These mazes were decorative features rather than puzzles. They sometimes followed the same patterns as the landscape mazes and mosaic pavements, but entirely new designs were also devised. These did not always have single pathways, but featured multiple routes and more than one entrance rather than paths that led to dead ends. Often, like the other patterns, or knots, laid out in plants, they were intended to be looked down upon from a raised path or terrace, or from an upper story, from which their design could be appreciated. They were usually formed from low-growing plants, often fragrant herbs and evergreens. The low box hedging that we normally associate with such designs was used to

surround the Medicis' maze in Castello, northern Italy, and perhaps in France, but it did not become widespread until later, and was probably not used in Britain before 1603. Sometimes mazes were constructed of trelliswork with climbing plants, or of bent willow wands, such as the mazes made in the Tuileries gardens in Paris in the 1560s. The willow (sometimes described as cherry) could have been woven into a trellis, or bent overhead to form the pergolas or tunnels that feature in some designs.

At Nonesuch, in 1599, the hedges were described as so high that no one could see over them. In the 17th century, hedges were sometimes considerably higher, the paths effectively being tree-bordered, or winding their way through thick blocks of shrubs instead of being neatly separated by uniform hedge barriers. English writer William Lawson, in *A New Orchard and Garden*, recommended planting a maze with fruiting shrubs and trees, to provide a crop as well as a recreational feature. He envisaged high hedging or trelliswork, because he advises that it be "well-framed a man's height so as to make your friend wander in gathering of berries till he cannot recover himself without your help."

*This design by Jan Vredeman de Vries is a very early example of a puzzle maze. Once found, the route is easily remembered, but if you miss it, you will find yourself back at the entrance.*

Higher barriers not only increased the sense of disorientation; they also gave those within the maze some privacy, a luxury often lacking in households where the nobility conducted almost every part of their lives in public – going to bed, getting up, bathing, and dressing were carried out surrounded by courtiers and servants. The maze was probably a place for confidences and intimacy, and for amorous encounters, but it could also be the setting for alfresco entertaining, for playing games, and making music.

### PUBLIC MAZES

Expenditure on the creation and upkeep of a maze was one way in which aristocrats flaunted their wealth and demonstrated their position, though they did not always restrict access to themselves and their guests. Some grand gardens were opened to local people, at least when the owner was not in residence. In the Netherlands,

# VERSAILLES FABLE MAZE

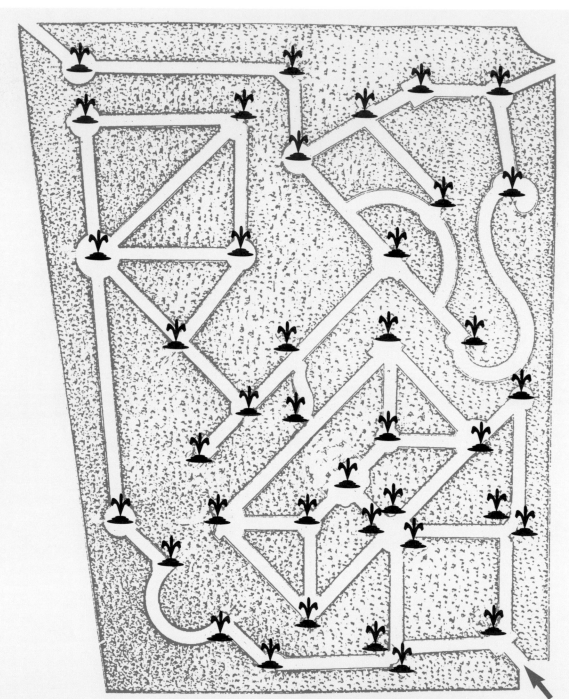

*L'ordre que tiennent les Compagnies depuis un jusques à 39.*

The Château de Versailles in its finest glory under Louis XIV contained a magnificent hedge maze. The paths were sometimes cut through very thick blocks of hedges that could be 20 feet (6 m) thick or more. By contrast, modern mazes have much thinner hedges of constant width. Although the layout of maze paths is not particularly difficult, a second, more challenging puzzle was hidden within. The hedges contained 39 fountains, arranged with statues, portraying the fables as originally told by Aesop. Each creature that spoke during the fable had a spout of water pouring out of its mouth. The challenge for visitors was to find a way through the maze, passing every fountain once and once only, and never crossing their route. One fountain lies in a dead end, so here you obviously have to retrace your route.

however, the more egalitarian people of Amsterdam had access to public mazes. The first was built in 1562, and in the 17th century, by which time it may have disappeared, two others were planted within a few years of each other, on the Princengracht and the neighboring Rozengracht. Interestingly, Dutch mazes often seem to have featured a tree at their center. Does this indicate a connection with turf mazes, some of which also contained a central tree – and a further link with the pre-Christian maypole dances?

## CUPID'S DOMAIN

The complexity of the maze was sometimes interpreted not as an allegory of life but as a symbol of the pains of love, with the hapless lover caught defenseless in its spirals. This, combined with their role as places of amorous dalliance, gained mazes the name and reputation of "labyrinths of love," and they were sometimes ornamented with statues of Cupid.

In 1669 an extensive maze was created for the Sun King Louis XIV in the gardens of the palace of Versailles. It was designed as a "wilderness," with broad paths through a thick wood rather than the narrow alleys of a hedge maze. Sadly, it was destroyed in 1775, but a detailed guide published in 1677 presents a plan and illustrates the statuary with which it was embellished. There were three ways in. The main entrance was flanked by two statues: Cupid, holding a ball of thread (the only symbol to link this maze with the Theseus story); and Aesop, the legendary figure from the 6th century BC, famous as author of the *Fables*. Each junction and angle in the paths had a fountain representing one of those fables, such as the race between the hare and the tortoise, with a jet of water to represent the speech of any animal that talks in them. The plan does not look very complex, but given the scale of the maze and the distances along each path, a person at its heart could still have experienced difficulty in finding the way out. To add complication and enjoyment, visitors were challenged to find a route on which they would see all of the thirty-nine fountains without passing any of them twice.

In the century that followed, numerous designs were published for such mazes with paths through woods or shrubbery. Sometimes they are symmetrical; sometimes they wander randomly. Increasingly they present paths that present a confusing choice: they offer a deliberate puzzle.

# THREE LANDS POINT HEDGE MAZE

**T**his maze in the Netherlands is one of the world's largest permanent hedge mazes. The maze paths are crossed in several places by rows of fountains, which temporarily block the paths, rising and falling seemingly at random. The paths also pass over and under wooden bridges. Your first challenge is to trace a route to the center, passing through any fountains and over or under any bridges. Your second challenge is also to trace a route to the center, but this time you may only pass over a bridge if you have been through precisely 3, 5, or 7 fountains. You can pass under the bridges as often as you like. There is a quick exit from the maze, which you should ignore.

### ABOVE

*Three Lands Point is situated at the southwestern tip of the Netherlands, where the country touches both Germany and Belgium. This is reflected in the overall shape of the maze, and its hedges represent the German eagle and two different lion symbols for Belgium and Holland.*

# MAZES TO GET LOST IN

On the banks of the River Thames, a dozen miles upstream from London, is a Tudor palace. Built originally by Cardinal Wolsey on monastic land and then presented by him to King Henry VIII in the 1520s, it became a royal residence. When Queen Mary II and her husband William of Orange came from Holland to reign as joint monarchs in 1689, they had its grounds refurbished to the Dutch taste. They introduced private gardens, a great vista across the parkland, and a "wilderness" to one side of the palace complex that contained four mazes: a labyrinth, two fairly simple semicircular mazes facing each other, and a trapezoid-shaped puzzle maze set between the angles of the paths. It was not the first puzzle maze. The diarist John Evelyn, a visitor to Italy earlier in the century, described seeing an "inextricable labyrinth" while on his travels, and Pope Clement X of the same period is reported to have enjoyed watching his servants trying to find their way out of the maze in his gardens at Altieri. However, the maze at Hampton Court is probably the earliest puzzle maze to have survived in its original form, and is now the world's best known and most copied maze.

### SOLVING A SIMPLE MAZE

William, who was also head of what is now the kingdom of the Netherlands (then the Dutch Republic), loved gardens – and mazes. There were already two mazes at the royal couple's Dutch palace at Het Loo: a hedge maze for William, and one consisting of walks with fountains and statuary for Mary. When Mary's sister Anne succeeded to the British throne in 1702, she had much of the formal gardens at Hampton Court uprooted. She did not like her brother-in-law and did not want to be reminded of him, but the puzzle maze remained. It is not a complicated puzzle. You can solve it by the trick of always following the hedge on one side. This technique may take you an unnecessarily long way around, but it is guaranteed to get you out of simple puzzle mazes.

The maze at the Villa Pisani in Stra, near Padua, in northern Italy, is another survivor,

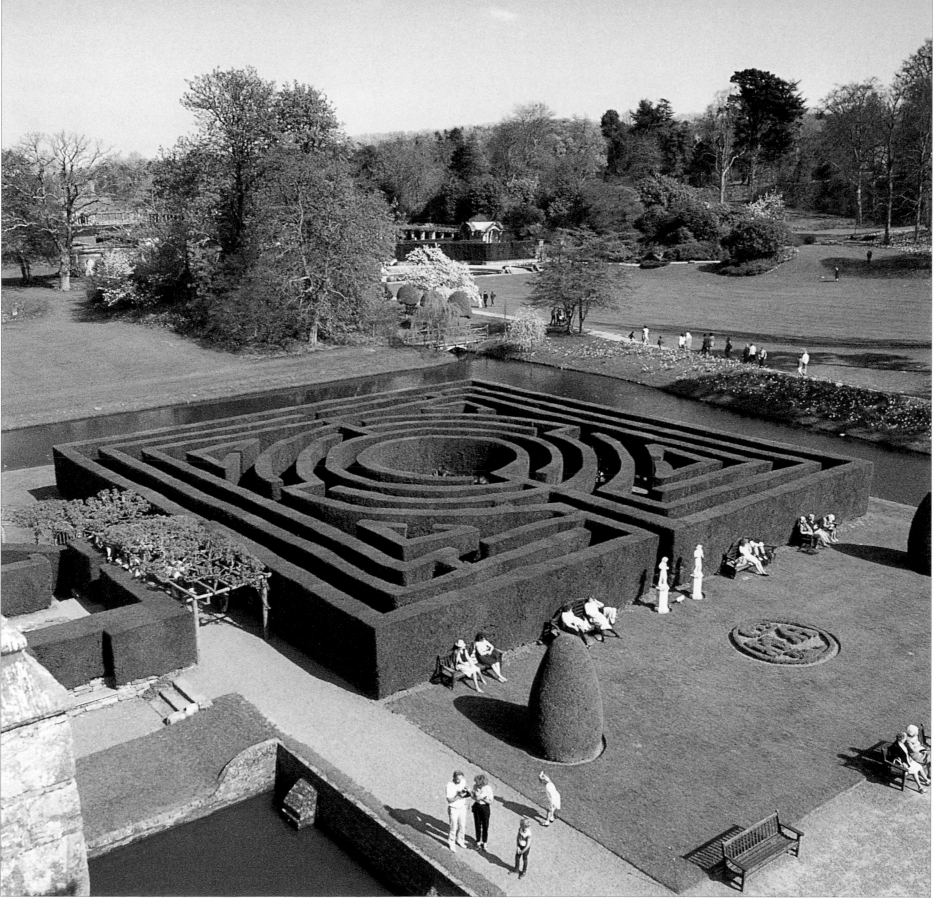

*The maze at Hampton Court, the royal palace on the Thames to the west of London, is probably the world's best known maze.*

The maze at Hampton Court is probably the most famous hedge maze in the world. It was planted as part of the gardens laid out for William of Orange between 1689 and 1695 by George London and Henry Wise. It was described with great wit in Jerome K. Jerome's novel Three Men in a Boat. Hampton Court Maze continues to attract hundreds of thousands of visitors each year.

On paper this is not a difficult maze to solve, but in reality many people get lost in it. Try to find your way around it using the Hand-on-Wall method. Imagine that you are walking around the maze with your right hand touching the hedge on your right-hand side. Follow the paths of the maze, always keeping your hand in contact with the hedge. Draw the hedge you are touching on an acetate sheet, not the path. You can use the same method with your left hand. We have placed six treasure chests in the paths of the maze. Which one do you not pass with either method?

# WILLIAMSBURG HEDGE MAZE

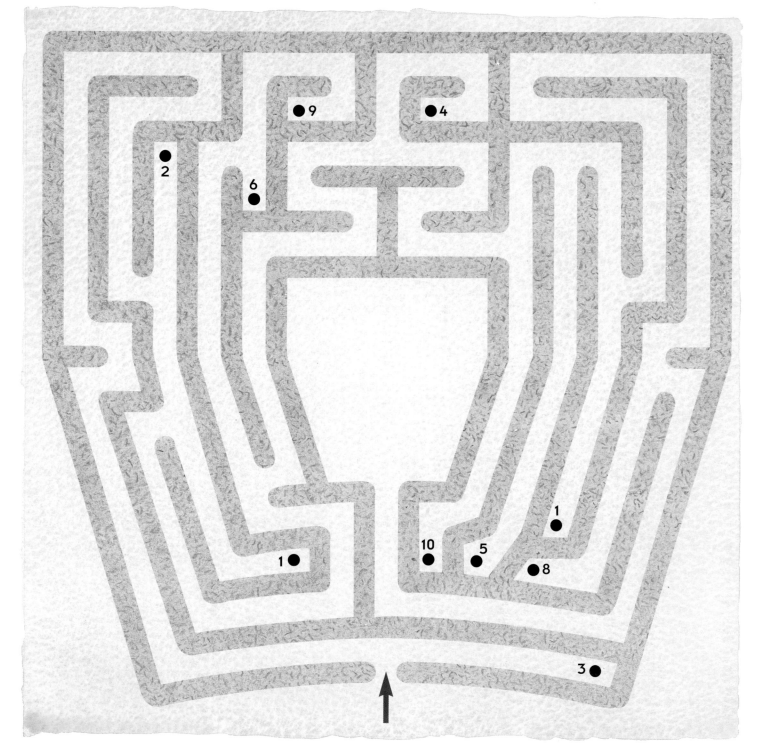

**W**illiamsburg Maze is probably the most famous hedge maze in North America. It was planted in holly in the grounds of the Governor's Palace in 1935 as part of the historic restoration of colonial Williamsburg. This is one of over a dozen mazes where the design has been copied or adapted from the maze at Hampton Court Palace. Accordingly, try solving this puzzle using both the right and left Hand-on-Wall methods, as explained in the instructions to Hampton Court Hedge Maze on the previous page. Follow the hedge wall in and out of each dead end until you reach the goal. In each of the dead ends, we have placed a bag, containing between one and ten gold coins, as indicated. With which method will you collect the most gold coins?

# VILLA PISANI TOWER MAZE

The maze in the gardens of the Villa Pisani at Stra, Italy, was planted circa 1720. Its goal is a tower in the center, surmounted by a statue of Minerva. Once visitors have reached the goal, they can climb the tower and survey the pattern of the maze laid out below them. This is probably Italy's most impressive maze, and is still maintained in excellent condition.

**BELOW**
*This engraving of the hedge maze at Villa Pisani makes the tower appear much wider than it really is.*

Although there is a small section of hedge in the bottom left corner that is detached from the rest, this maze can still be solved using the Hand-on-Wall method. Try that first, ignoring the spears that we have added. Next, trace a route that allows you to pick up all ten spears. They are very sharp, so you can only pick up a spear by approaching it from its shaft.

although not as old as Hampton Court. It is an elegant maze, with plenty of opportunities to get lost. It is still solvable by the trick explained above, but leads visitors in and out of numerous dead-ends if they apply it precisely and persistently.

### MEANDERING MAZES

Compact geometrical designs, such as those of Hampton Court and Stra, provided lively formal puzzles. But other designers, influenced perhaps by the Versailles style, produced concepts that meandered irregularly, apparently providing an entertaining promenade rather than a true puzzle. Plans for these appear among the many offered by Batty Langley in his *New Principles of Gardening* in 1728. By contrast, Stephen Switzer, who published the gardening book *Ichonographia Rustica* in 1742, set out to confuse as much as possible. However, the tediously long and repetitive paths of a design such as Switzer's could scarcely be called a satisfying puzzle.

## GLENDURGAN HEDGE MAZE

The maze at Glendurgan House is among England's earliest surviving hedge mazes. Planted in laurel, its inspired position on one side of a narrow valley gives an almost bird's-eye view of its sinuous rows of hedges when you stand on the bank opposite. It was designed by Alfred Fox in 1833, and its free-flowing design is quite unlike the formal patterns of traditional garden mazes. The design is derived from that of a maze that formerly existed in Sidney Gardens at Bath, a fashionable place of entertainment in the late 18th and early 19th centuries, when Jane Austen was among its visitors.

### BELOW
*The maze at Glendurgan is situated on a slope, and its pattern is easy to see from the hillside opposite.*

# CHEVENING HEDGE MAZE

etween 1818 and 1830, the 4th Earl of Stanhope planted a yew hedge maze at Chevening House in England from a design by the 2nd Earl, who was an eminent mathematician. Unfortunately, this maze lies in private grounds and so cannot be visited by the public. The design was highly innovative, taking maze puzzlement to the most complex two-dimensional form possible. Unlike earlier historic hedge mazes, you cannot solve Chevening Maze using the Hand-on-Wall method, since this will simply take you right around the maze and back out the entrance without ever reaching the central goal. As an extra puzzle, we have added chevrons, which indicate that a path is one-way only – you must never go the wrong way along a one-way path. You can, of course, complete the maze ignoring the chevrons if you wish.

**BELOW**
*The maze at Chevening is a private maze, but its elegant form introduced a new era of puzzlement to maze design.*

# ITALIANATE MAZE

This maze was created at Capel Manor, England, in 1991 to reflect the enthusiasm for Italian gardens that seized Europe in the 1830s and 40s. Several Italianate mazes were created at that time, and this modern design brings together characteristic elements from all those mazes. It has a confusing network of holly hedges, with a beautiful two-tier fountain and four statues within the central courtyard, the goal of the maze.

As an extra puzzle, we have added several rows of fountains and several rows of flames, which block the paths of the maze at intervals. Whenever all the fountains are up, all the flames are down, and vice versa. Assume that all the fountains are up when you first enter the maze. Hidden in the maze are also some pressure pads. Whenever you cross a pressure pad, all the flames and fountains change, from being up to down, or down to up. Find a way to reach the central goal without going through any of the flames or fountains. First, however, you can try to solve the maze ignoring the extra puzzle elements that we have added to it.

Pressure pads

Rows of fountains

Rows of flames

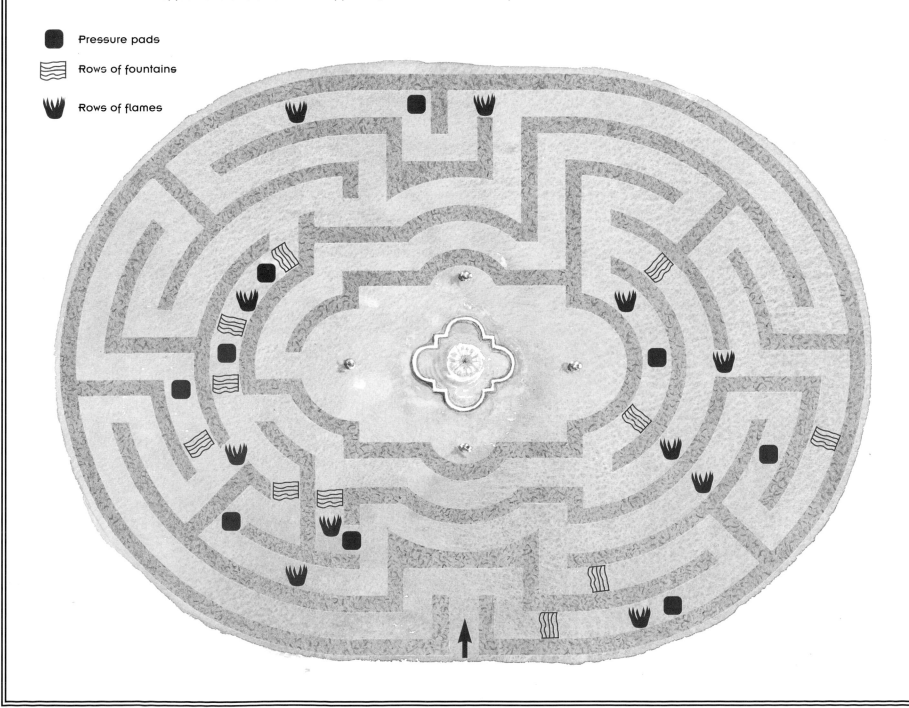

# SAFFRON WALDEN HEDGE MAZE

The hedge maze at Saffron Walden in southern England was first planted in 1839. It is of an Italianate design, and was originally embellished with statues and a viewing platform at the center. It was a popular place to visit in the 19th century, but during the first half of the 20th century it was neglected and became overgrown. The original hedges were eventually uprooted in 1984, but the maze has been replanted in an exact copy of the original.

## COMPLICATING THE PUZZLE

It was not for more than a century after the planting of the Hampton Court maze that a way was discovered of creating a puzzle that could not be solved by simple methods (such as the Hand-on-Wall method that you will learn when trying to solve some of the mazes in this book). Credit for this invention should probably be awarded to an aristocratic English mathematician, the second Earl of Stanhope, who designed at least three mazes. The one that he made between 1816 and 1830 survives at Chevening House in Kent. This is now the country residence of the British Foreign Secretary, and strict security arrangements prevent the public from visiting it, but a plan is enough to demonstrate the principles on which it is based. The barriers of the earlier mazes were all connected, except perhaps for sections that had no real effect on the route. Chevening's scheme isolates the containing hedges from the central core, and therefore complicates the pattern.

The landscape style of gardening that was introduced in Britain in the 18th century, and then adopted elsewhere, had little place for the formality of hedge mazes. However, they retained their popularity as a feature of public gardens, such as the Sidney Gardens in Bath, which were a fashionable haunt of the early 19th century, and as an attraction in the tea-gardens that grew up as places of relaxation and amusement on the outskirts of London. Later a revival of interest in Italian Renaissance gardens brought the mazes back into vogue. When the first civic public parks were created in the middle of the 19th century, they sometimes featured mazes, but because they take time to grow and need regular maintenance, they were mainly to be found in the gardens of grand houses.

# CHATSWORTH HEDGE MAZE

The maze at Chatsworth House, England, has one of the most magnificent landscape settings of any hedge maze in the world. A huge conservatory built in the 19th century formerly stood on its site, so it is not an old maze. However, it was planted from an old design, found in the household papers, that may at one time have existed elswehere on the estate.

## ABOVE

*In the past, the public were not admitted to Chatsworth Maze, but could view it from the surrounding gardens. In recent years, however, visitors have been welcomed.*

For this puzzle, we have invented eight secret tunnels under the maze. Each tunnel has two entrance points. Numbered dice indicate the entrances to the different tunnel systems. So, for example, the entrances to tunnel number seven are indicated with dice bearing a total of seven dots. If you enter tunnel seven at one entrance, you can travel beneath the maze directly to its other entrance, where you can exit the tunnel and rejoin the maze above ground. Your objective is to travel once through each of the tunnels to reach the central goal, without using the same maze path above ground more than once. First, however, you can try to solve the maze as it stands, ignoring the extra puzzle element we have added.

# RUSSBOROUGH HEDGE MAZE

The formal hedge maze at Russborough House in Ireland has a pillar at its center topped by the figure of Cupid, making the goal tantalizingly visible to those negotiating the paths of the maze. For this two-dimensional plan of the maze, we have represented the goal with a diamond, which conceals a clue to the identity of the maze's owner, since Sir Alfred Beit's family were early pioneers in the world diamond industry. As you make your way to the central diamond, you must pass rubies and sapphires alternately. Since they don't belong to you, of course, you must leave them where they are! Remember, you can also ignore the extra puzzle of the sapphires and rubies if you wish, and wander the paths of the maze as they stand.

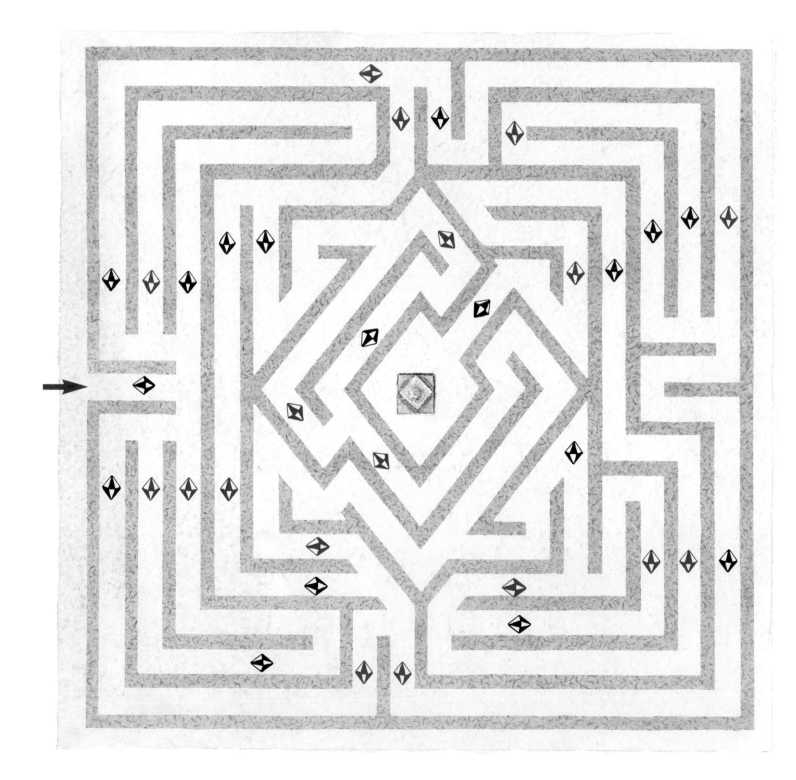

# NEW HARMONY
# HEDGE MAZE

The maze at New Harmony, Indiana, was planted in 1939 to commemorate the original vine hedge maze that stood there from 1814–50. The original maze was planted by the Harmony Society, a German protestant sect that emigrated to America in 1803–4. The maze was intended to symbolize the spirit of their movement and the difficulty of achieving harmony. It fell into neglect in the 1840s. The plan shown here is of the existing New Harmony Maze. Although it looks deceptively like a unicursal labyrinth, it is not. The path can lead to the surrounding lawns or into two dead ends, and there is an extra trap for those trying to leave the center. You can choose any of the three paths to enter the maze.

## THE INDIANA MAZE

Neither private nor public mazes seem to have been popular in the early history of the United States. An exception, however, is a maze that was planted in Indiana by a community of German immigrants. This group, which arrived in America in 1803–4, was a Protestant sect led by its founder George Rapp. They settled first at Harmonie (now Harmony) in Pennsylvania, and a decade later moved to establish another settlement, named New Harmony, in Indiana. Here they made a maze of vines and shrubs. We do not know whether it was a unicursal labyrinth or a simple puzzle maze – it would have been too early to have featured Stanhope's refinements – but we

### RIGHT
*The maze at Afton Villa, Louisiana, is a beautiful American example of a modern hedge maze.*

# MURRAY MAZE

Scone was the place of coronation of Scottish kings and queens for many centuries, before the ancient kingdom of Scotland joined with England to form the United Kingdom. Scone Palace was built on this historic site. This beech hedge maze at Scone is planted in green beech and copper beech to produce a tartan effect. It is in the shape of the five-pointed "Murray Star," the heraldic symbol of the family who commissioned the maze.

We have placed a Scottish thistle in each of the 27 "cells" of the maze. Pick up as many thistles as you can, while tracing a path from the entrance to the goal at the center that does not cross over itself. You must use two different paths to enter and leave each cell within the design. How many thistles is it possible to pick up? You can, of course, ignore the thistles and solve the maze as it stands if you wish.

do have a description of it in 1822 as: "a most elegant flower garden with various hedgerows disposed in such a manner as to puzzle people to get into the little temple, emblematic of Harmony, in the middle. The Labyrinth represents the difficulty of arriving at harmony. The temple is rough on the exterior, showing that, at a distance, it has no allurements, but it is smooth and beautiful within to show the beauty of harmony when once attained."

While European garden mazes were becoming decorative amusements, here was a maze rooted in a symbolic purpose. The Rappites moved on to Economy (now Ambridge) in Pennsylvania, and in 1824 the second Harmony became the base for a Utopian colony established by the Scottish socialist Robert Owen, for whom the maze held less meaning. It disappeared around the middle of the 19th century. In the mid-20th century, however, a new hedge maze was planted to commemorate the Rappite settlers, again with an externally simple central structure. It combines its puzzlement with a feeling of peaceful tranquility appropriate to its significance.

**ABOVE**

*The maze in the gardens of Villa Giusta at Verona in northern Italy has a fountain as its central goal.*

**LEFT**

*The maze at Margam Abbey in Wales has a castellated perimeter that is a reminder of Roman mosaic mazes.*

### RESTORATIONS AND REVIVALS

A British designer of several 19th-century mazes was a former naval officer, Lt. W.H. Nesfield. He created a maze for the Royal Horticultural Society's gardens (then in South Kensington, London) in about 1862, reportedly at the suggestion of Prince Albert, the husband of Queen Victoria. Some of the great houses restored old mazes or established new ones: for example, at Hatfield House in Hertfordshire (built in 1611), a large hedge maze was created, reputedly for a visit by Queen Victoria; and when American-born newspaper proprietor Viscount William Waldorf Astor bought Hever Castle in Edenbridge, Kent, at the beginning of the 20th century, he had a maze planted to match its Tudor history.

Overseas visitors to Hampton Court and Britons traveling to far-flung corners of what was then the British Empire carried memories of that maze with them, and made copies or adaptations of it. One such was Miss Cornelia Warren of Waltham, Massachusetts, who planted a copy of the Hampton Court design in 1896, in hedges of arborvitae, though rounding its angles into gentler curves.

The two world wars and social changes of the 20th century saw many existing hedge mazes becoming neglected or even uprooted. Mazes were to be found in puzzle books rather than in gardens. But the latter decades of the 20th century have seen a revival of the garden maze, a new interest in the traditions and significance of ancient labyrinths, and the development of new forms of the maze as commercial entertainment.

BELOW

*Once visitors have reached the center of the maze, they climb several steps to a raised viewing platform, from which they can enjoy an aerial view of its magnificent design.*

# SAXON HERB MAZE

This maze, on a herb farm in England, is set within an earth rampart that suggests Saxon fortifications. It has a four-fold rotational symmetry, reflecting the four main categories of herbs — culinary, medicinal, aromatic, and decorative. Its beech hedges portray four mythical sea creatures derived from an 8th-century illuminated manuscript, and the eye of each is planted with aromatic herbs. The goal is raised on a central tump.

As an extra puzzle element, we have placed beds of herbs around the paths of the maze. Find a way to travel around the maze, picking up all seven herbs once each. You need to collect parsley, sage, rosemary, thyme, dill, marjoram, and basil. You cannot turn back on yourself, nor may you use any maze path more than once. As always, you can also solve the maze as it stands, without referring to the extra puzzle we have added to its design.

# CREATION MAZE

This maze at Värmlands Säby in Sweden is planted in amlanchier, a flowering shrub that adds seasonal variety for visitors. Contained within the archetypal symbol of the egg, it contains a host of other symbols illustrating two scenarios. The first is the Garden of Eden, with a central tree of knowledge, Adam and Eve on each side, the serpent below, and 22 different animals. The second is the story of the Minotaur, featuring Ariadne and several other figures. There is also a falcon as the symbol of the family who commissioned the maze.

Choose either one of the two entrances, then trace your way through the maze to the goal at the top of the tree near the apex of the design. As an added puzzle, we have colored some sections of the path through the tree to represent apples. Trace a route to the goal of the maze that passes each apple once. Your route must never use the same pathway more than once. You can, of course, solve the maze ignoring the extra rules we have added.

# AMAZING
# MODERN MAZES

For a long time the walkable maze was either a flat pavement or a path through growing shrubs, usually in a relatively geometric pattern. Occasional exceptions, such as the 19th-century maze at Glendurgan in Cornwall, England, bent and twisted in an apparently random fashion. In books and magazines, however, and sometimes in toys, new approaches were tried. As far back as the 17th century, Italian architect Francesco Segala produced some imaginative maze drawings that fit the paths within the forms of people and objects. Later, games published in children's books and magazines used picture-story mazes in which the player was challenged to find a way through evil enchanted forests to rescue a hostage, or perhaps just to get a pig safely to market. Today, such figurative elements have been taken up both literally and symbolically as part of the increasing diversity and innovation of modern maze-making.

## THE WORLD'S LONGEST MAZE

One of the first innovations was a complicated serpentine pattern of paths dug as trenches, varying from a shallow 1 ft 6 in (45 cm) to 6 ft (1.8 m) deep, in a field in Somerset, England. It was built over the course of a year in the early 1970s by Englishman Greg Bright, with the help of friends. Bright went on to make more conventional mazes and to produce puzzle books, but he is best known for the huge maze he created in the grounds of Longleat House, near Warminster in Wiltshire, commissioned by Lord Weymouth (now the Marquis of Bath). Opened in 1978, the Longleat maze has swirling paths like those of Bright's first maze, but it is made of yew

**ABOVE**

*The Nautical Maze at Legoland amusement park in England echoes the colors of naval signaling flags.*

**RIGHT**

*This huge hedge maze was the first of the many mazes commissioned for Longleat House in southern England.*

hedges and uses a number of bridges to link parts that are totally self-enclosed. Although huge, it is not quite the largest permanent maze in the world. That honor belongs to the relatively simple design at Ruullo in the Netherlands, which is based on the maze at Hampton Court, but has wide paths lined with lawns between the hedges, quite different from the compact alleys of the traditional maze. However, Longleat has a greater length of path, and the visitor needs to allow an hour to solve it, plus time to solve the other three mazes that have been built there.

**PREVIOUS PAGE**

*This wooden maze at Kyoto in Japan has numerous bridges to create a three-dimensional puzzle.*

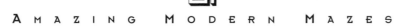

# LONGLEAT
# HEDGE MAZE

Longleat House is an Elizabethan residence in the south of England. The world's longest hedge maze, featured here, can be found within its grounds, but Longleat also boasts the distinction of having the greatest concentration of landscape mazes. The hedge maze features six bridges, which create a three-dimensional puzzle. Spiral junctions are intended to add confusion by repetition, and elongated fork junctions are cunningly used, since visitors are thought to prefer to "conserve their momentum" rather than make U-turns. The whirling lines and the lack of any rectangular grid add further disorientation. The goal is at the center, where there is a viewing platform.

**ABOVE**

*This is the world's longest hedge maze. It was planted in yew and opened in 1978 at Longleat House.*

## SYMBOLIC MAZES

Maze designs with symbolic and figurative elements are the specialty of former British diplomat Randoll Coate, who also devised two of the mazes at Longleat. His mazes consist of multiple images superimposed to convey many layers of meaning, visible from an overlooking viewpoint, or revealed in their plan. Coate and Adrian Fisher (designer of the puzzles and many of the mazes in this book), and for a brief period landscape gardener Graham Burgess (who is the designer of one of the Longleat mazes), joined forces in the 1980s to produce a range of figurative designs that formed overall shapes, such as a dragon, footprints, and heraldic symbols. A dream by the Church of England's leading prelate, the Archbishop of Canterbury, was translated into a design full of Christian symbolism; and a maze celebrating the Beatles won an international gold medal for innovation.

**ABOVE**

*The Tudor Rose Maze fills the main courtyard of Kentwell Hall in Suffolk, England. This is the world's largest brick pavement maze.*

**LEFT**

*The maze at Blenheim Palace, situated in the south of England, is the world's largest symbolic hedge maze. Its yew hedges contain images of a firing cannon, cannon balls, banners, flags, and trumpets, in celebration of the Duke of Marlborough's military victories.*

# LEEDS CASTLE HEDGE MAZE

Leeds Castle dates back to the 9th century and has been the royal castle of three kings and queens of England. Opened in 1988, this hedge maze has the formality and symmetry of early garden mazes, in character with its historic site, but also presents an extremely challenging puzzle. It employs symbolic elements, rising to a central tower from which visitors can see the shapes of a crown and a communion chalice within the paths. The central mound symbolizes a communion host. A grotto beneath the mound is decorated with thousands of sea shells and leads to a long underground exit tunnel. As an extra puzzle, we have placed sea shells along the pathways of the maze. Find a route through the maze that allows you to pick up as many shells as possible. However, you must take a route that never crosses over itself. You will find that there are some sea shells that you cannot collect – how many? If you wish, you can also solve the maze ignoring the extra puzzle elements we have added.

# TWO GRAY HILLS COLOR MAZE

This maze is based on a Native American rug design. Within the maze, there is a single thread that runs out to the edge of the carpet, to allow the Spirit of the Rug to come and go freely. The maze paths are red, brown, and yellow. The other colors are mainly for decoration. Enter along the red path from the perimeter, then change path color each time you pass through a black diamond junction square. Your goal is the central diamond.

**RIGHT**
*Visitors to the Two Gray Hills Color Maze at San Antonio in the United States find this small maze surprisingly complex.*

# THREE FLAGS COLOR MAZE

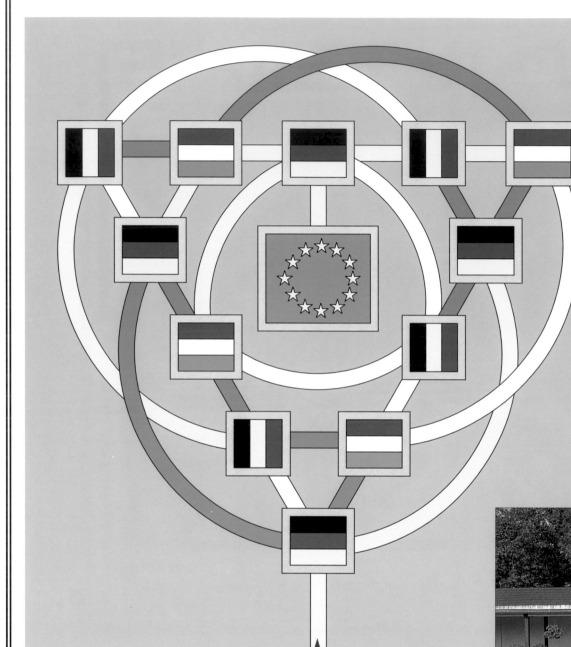

This color maze lies at the meeting point of the borders of Germany, Belgium, and the Netherlands, and so contains all three countries' flags in its design. The maze paths are yellow, green, and white, and they weave over and under each other in places. Enter along the yellow path from the perimeter, then change path color each time you pass through a flag. Your goal is the central flag of the European Community.

**RIGHT**
*Three Flags Color Maze is located at the exit from Three Land's Point Hedge Maze in the Netherlands.*

## WOODEN MAZES

Another innovation is the wooden maze, first built in Wanaka, New Zealand, in 1973 by Stuart Landsborough. He went on to build others in Australia, New Zealand, North America, and Japan. Extremely popular, more than 150 examples were erected in Japan during the 1980s. Designed as amusement attractions, they often incorporated bridges, towers, and covered areas to add to their confusion, and visitors were frequently invited to "run" them against the clock – names of the day's fastest runners being displayed to bring them instant fame. Sometimes cards were issued, which had to be time-stamped when the visitor reached particular features, and often in a particular sequence.

Such mazes are a far cry from the ancient labyrinths of Rome and Scandinavia, but commercial mazes have provided a major impetus in the development of innovative forms. In the past, an owner might charge a small amount to walk a maze – one penny (in Britain's pre-decimal coinage) at Hampton Court. At fairgrounds, the "Hall of Mirrors" offered a money-making variation of the puzzle that depended on optical illusion rather than physical barriers to disorient. As a result, much more sophisticated mirror mazes are now being built. Increased family leisure and spending power has produced a vast

# DRAGON MIRROR MAZE

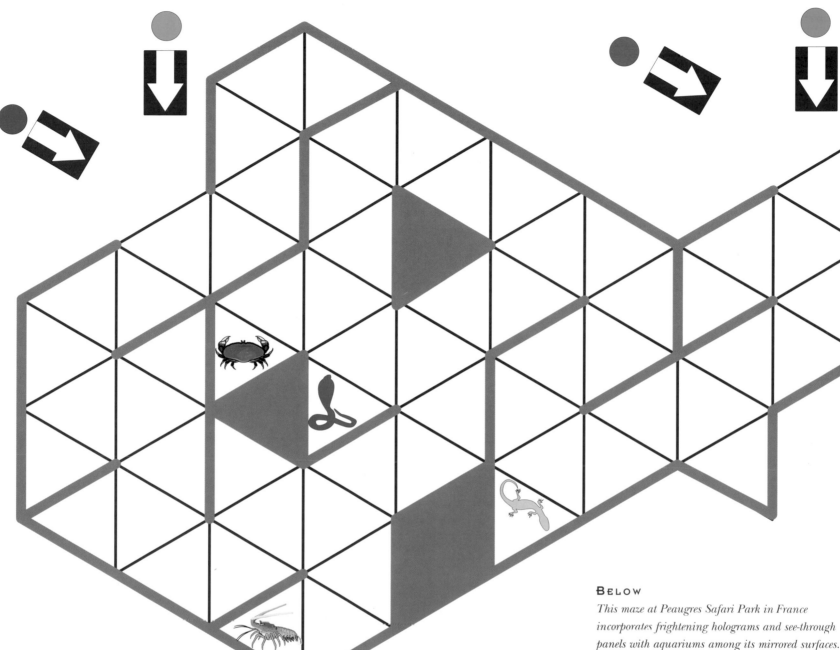

**BELOW**

*This maze at Peaugres Safari Park in France incorporates frightening holograms and see-through panels with aquariums among its mirrored surfaces.*

Mirror mazes work by producing a multitude of reflections of the same image that are bounced from mirror to mirror so that the viewer cannot see which is the original, and often cannot see the original at all. This intriguing mirror maze in a French safari park is the climax of a major exhibit that contains live crocodiles, pythons, scorpions, and bats. In real life, the creatures are behind glass, though here we have allowed four of them to escape into the maze. We have used colored circles to show the positions of four observers standing outside of the maze. The sightline of each of observer is indicated with an arrow. Each observer can see one of the creatures through the reflections of the mirrors. To trace the line of sight of each observer, draw a straight line to the first mirror, then turn the sight line at an angle of 45 degrees, and continue straight to the next mirror, and so on. Which observer can see which creature?

# MAZE OF THE PLANETS

The Maze of the Planets is a wooden maze constructed in Michigan in the United States. Its bridges and circling paths look like a giant image of the planet Saturn when seen from above, and the bridges give it a three-dimensional complexity.

We have added a further challenge to solving the original puzzle. Your task is to travel to the center of the maze, never using any path more than once. We have placed some black holes within the maze, which in outer space are, of course, extremely dangerous. However, if you tip a bucketful of fairy dust into a black hole, you fill the hole so that you can get past it. Piles of fairy dust can be found at various points around the maze. You can carry two buckets at once, whether full or empty, and each bucket can hold enough fairy dust to fill one black hole. However, fairy dust is so heavy that you cannot carry any of it over any of the bridges. You can also, of course, ignore all the black holes and fairy dust, and solve the maze as it stands.

**BELOW**

*The four bridges represent Saturn's rings. The large central goal provides space for a small color maze and other activities.*

# ARCHERY MAZE

**T**his maze was part of a maze exhibition in 1995 at the Chicago Museum of Science and Industry. Start at the arrow at the center of the bottom row, and proceed for as many squares as you choose in the given direction.

Once you have stopped, change direction and move according to the direction of your new arrow, again for as far as you wish. Continue in this way. Your goal is to reach the central checkerboard square.

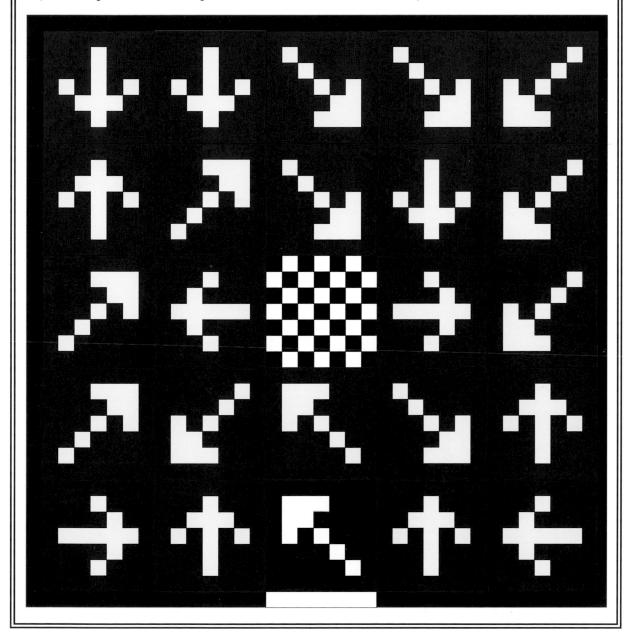

new industry, of which mazes are a part, both as entertainment at amusement parks and historic places, and as attractions in themselves.

### EVER-CHANGING MAZES

The United States continues the carnival tradition with portable mazes, designed by Kelly Fernandi. These consist of poles and vinyl plastic barriers that can be set up as temporary installations, or used to alter the patterns of existing mazes to produce more complicated puzzles for visitors to solve. Temporary mazes have also been made out of automobiles, mirrors, and colored strips and blocks. In Montreal, an interactive indoor maze (the work of Guy and Paul Chartier) is equipped with a seasonally changing theme and staffed by

storytellers and animators. The United States has original versions of the wooden maze, and at the opposite end of the maze spectrum are the turf labyrinths and earth mazes designed by Alex Champion. These are often intended for spiritual purposes, in suitable settings, such as the Prairie Peace Park in Lincoln, Nebraska. There are a number of examples in California.

## KNIGHT'S MAZE

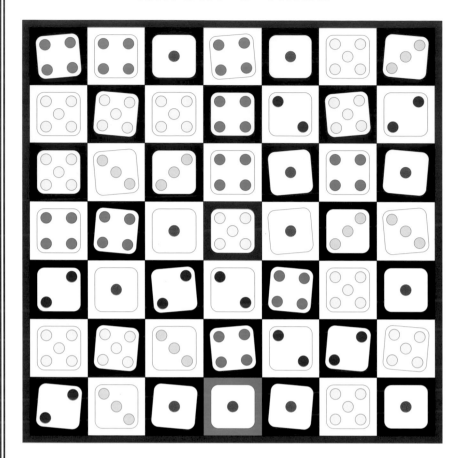

## BISHOP'S MAZE

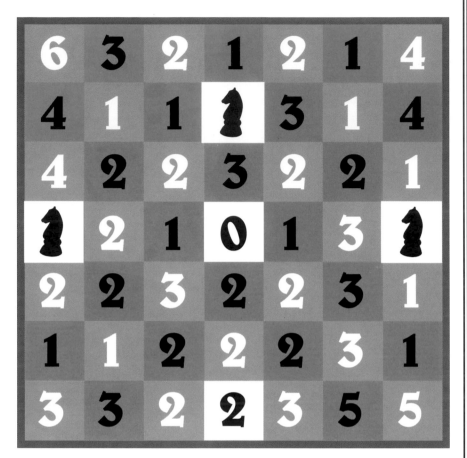

A maze does not have to consist of a continuous path. In these two mazes, your moves are regulated by the rules of chess, rather than barriers. This unusual maze combines the knight's move in chess with a dice game. A knight can move two squares to the side, then one square forward or backward, or two squares forward or backward and then one square to the side. Start at the number one at the center of the bottom row. Make a knight's move to reach a number two dice. Make a knight's move again to reach a number three, then four, then five. Continue in this way, traveling from one to five in sequence, until you reach the central number five square.

A bishop in chess moves diagonally only, but can move any number of squares. Here, however, the number of squares you can move is determined by the number given in the square you start from, and you must always stay on the checkerboard. There are also three knight's squares, indicated with the horse chess symbol. When you reach one of these, make one knight's move, then revert to the bishop's move. You will find that every time you make a knight's move, you change square color. Start at number two at the center of the bottom row. The goal is the central zero square. Remember, the square you land on dictates the distance of your next move.

Modern mazes exist alongside imposing residences and in individual backyards, on the walkways of city centers and shopping malls, in vacation resorts and places of entertainment, and in open country. Bridges are often included as part of the puzzle, or to offer vistas across mazes of symbolic design. Japanese mazes sometimes use one-way gates along the paths. Control structures devised by Fisher take the form of "foaming fountain" gates and "parting waterfalls" that bar the way intermittently and not always in the same direction.

### LEFT

*In this temporary maze, a driver had to reach the goal, then reverse and drive out as quickly as possible. However, while the competitor drove toward the goal, other drivers had changed the path out of the maze by moving some of the cars.*

### EDUCATIONAL MAZES

A device at the Darwin Maze at Edinburgh Zoo in Scotland operates by the selection of human characteristics, which teaches the theory of

# SNOWFLAKE COLOR MAZE

Sequential color mazes of this kind are particularly ingenious, since it is possible to force unusual routes across the same junction as many as two or three times before reaching the goal. By reversing the color sequence, a second and completely different puzzle maze emerges. The hexagonal array of paths and junctions allows the maximum number of colored paths to meet at each junction.

Your goal is the central star. You must change path color when you pass through each star on your way to the goal in the strict sequence of Red–Blue–Yellow repeatedly. For example, enter on the red path leading to 7, then take a blue path to 4, then a yellow path to 5, then a red path to 6, and so on. As a variant, try any of the other entrances and the color sequence Red–Yellow–Blue.

evolution as well as being fun. Another, created for Britain's Royal National Institute for the Blind, helps young visually impaired people develop their sensory and orienting skills as well as providing an entertaining puzzle for both unsighted and sighted. It was originally built in response to a television challenge program, after consultation on design with the youngsters themselves. Scent, texture, sound, space, and changes of level offer guidance and challenges, which are used in a three-year plan of mobility training exercises.

Pavement mazes often work in colored brick or specially designed paving stones. "Bridges" can be included – you will find yourself using them on the flat plans in this book. Many other rules can be introduced to control progress around the maze; for example, following colored paths where

LEFT

*The small scale of most brick puzzle mazes makes them ideal for areas where a larger landscape maze would be unsuitable.*

# ONE-WAY RAILWAY MAZE

**M**azes with rules sometimes share a common characteristic, even though their appearance may differ widely. One typical trick is that of reversing the polarity of a maze path; the same idea underlies color mazes that flip between two path colors, and one-way mazes that rely on an underlying clockwise or counterclockwise flow. A change of polarity is essential to reach the

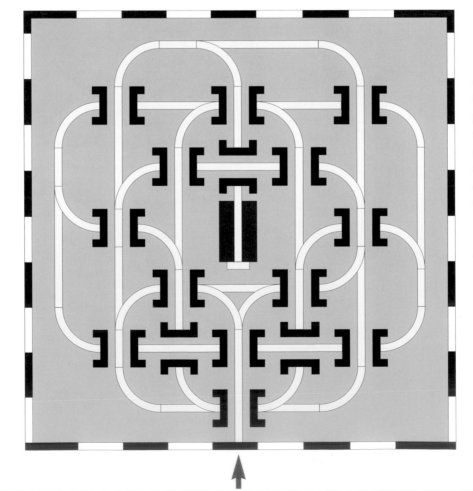

goal of this One-way Railway Maze. Start at the foot of the design and proceed forward only, over and under the bridges. Your first objective is to reach the final station at the center of the maze. Your second objective is again to reach the final station, but this time you must pass over and under an equal number of bridges on your way to the final destination.

# NEW ORLEANS COLOR MAZE

This maze design is based on the logo of the Louisiana Children's Museum. The logo consists of two little Cajun houses with the moon above, in the deep blue night sky of the American South. The maze paths are yellow, green, and gray, and connect with various irregular windows and doors. Start at either of the two doors, and change path color each time you pass through a window square. Your goal is the crescent moon.

**RIGHT**

*This color maze was laid out in a street for passersby to test before being installed in the Louisiana Children's Museum.*

# ZIGGURAT COLOR MAZE

**T**his color maze was designed for the New York Hall of Science for a special maze exhibition in 1993. The idea was to create a highly colorful design that would be instantly recognizable as a maze, and yet contained a puzzle that would take some five or six minutes to solve. Enter the maze on the yellow path, then change path color from yellow to white or white to yellow each time you pass through a red junction square. Your goal is the central red square.

LEFT

*The Ziggurat Color Maze being tested by children in preparation for its appearance at a maze exhibition in the United States.*

ABOVE

*The Multi-Sensory Mobility Maze was built to help visually impaired people develop their sensory and orientation skills.*

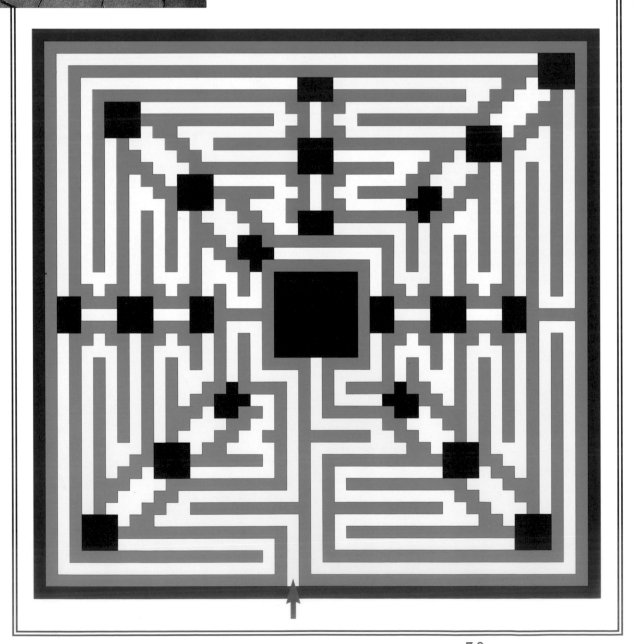

you can only change color in a certain sequence. Some "color mazes" apply this principle to compact formal shapes in which directional, mathematical, alphabetical, and other rules must be observed, and have found a useful place in some schools. Along with the challenge to comprehension and interpretation, this use of literacy, numerical, and orienting skills has obvious educational value. However, schools with such mazes in their yards found that they play an even more valuable role in social development, and in stimulating the children to develop their own rules.

## MAIZE MAZES

In the United States, a more traditional approach to maze-making evolved into the thoroughly modern "amazing maize mazes," three times winner of the record for the world's largest maze. These huge structures cut a pattern through growing fields of maize to provide a summer attraction that disappears when the corn is harvested. Developed by Fisher in collaboration with Broadway producer Don Frantz, they incorporate bridges and controls of various kinds, along with music throughout the maze, and various effects suitable to their subject. A "maze master" in a tall tower communicates with visitors

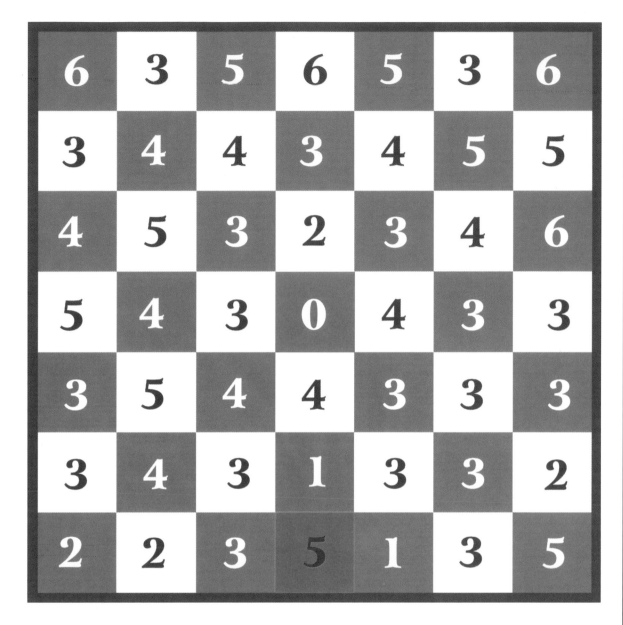

## NUMBER MAZE

**P**art of the challenge when devising a maze puzzle is to make the problem seem deceptively simple. Here, there is just an array of numbers, and one simple rule. The actual routes that can be navigated around this puzzle are anything but direct, and the shortest solution proves remarkably long. Start at the number five at the center of the bottom row. Move precisely that number of squares in any straight line, backward, forward, sideways, or diagonal. You must always stay on the checkerboard. Whatever square you land on dictates the distance of your next move. Your goal is the central zero square.

| 6 | 3 | 5 | 6 | 5 | 3 | 6 |
|---|---|---|---|---|---|---|
| 3 | 4 | 4 | 3 | 4 | 5 | 5 |
| 4 | 5 | 3 | 2 | 3 | 4 | 6 |
| 5 | 4 | 3 | 0 | 4 | 3 | 3 |
| 3 | 5 | 4 | 4 | 3 | 3 | 3 |
| 3 | 4 | 3 | 1 | 3 | 3 | 2 |
| 2 | 2 | 3 | 5 | 1 | 3 | 5 |

through speaking tubes, giving advice and encouragement to help them on their way – or just occasionally mislead them!

In schoolyard or cornfield, historic garden or shopping mall, mazes are adding stimulus and fun to life. Other mazes offer an opportunity for quiet contemplation or to explore personal and spiritual development. All are rooted in an ancient tradition that is still evolving. Enjoy them in your own way.

### RIGHT

*The first of the Amazing Maize Mazes in the United States was built in the shape of a giant stegosaurus dinosaur.*

# GOLDEN HINDE AMAZING MAIZE MAZE

**W**hen created in an American maize cornfield in 1995, this four-acre maze broke the Guinness record for the world's largest maze. The maze design portrays Sir Francis Drake's famous ship the Golden Hinde of 1578, on which he circumnavigated the world. The paths of the maze were cut through a vast field of corn, and like all the maize mazes, there was music piped throughout. Speaking tubes at various points allowed visitors who got into difficulties to contact the Maze Master, overseeing all from the top of a scaffold tower, for advice – helpful if they were getting really desperate, or unhelpful if he thought that would add to their fun! "Sea spray" from hoses sometimes washed over the "decks" to make the atmosphere more nautical in this ocean of corn. Over 25,000 visitors solved the maze over a series of four weekends, exiting it via a victory bridge from which they could survey the giant maze they had just conquered.

**ABOVE**

*The Golden Hinde Amazing Maize Maze was constructed at Shippensburg, Pennsylvania, as part of the 1995 Corn Festival.*

Sail the seas of corn to reach the heart of the ship, wherein lies the treasure you seek. There is a bridge at the top of the main mast, where paths cross over and under each other. Once you have found your goal, the only way off the ship is by walking the plank!

**T**his three-acre maze was built alongside the line of the Strasburg railroad in Amish country in central Pennsylvania. It was based on old steam locomotives that once ran along the railroad. Visitors were carried to and from the maze on an old steam train, the snorting engines of which could be heard by them as they tried to solve the maze. Clouds of smoke sometimes drifted over the paths of the maze, completing the experience. Enter through the gap on the left and aim at the center front of the boiler. A bridge provides a quick exit.

**RIGHT**
*The Paradise Valley
Amazing Maize Maze,
as seen from the air.*

# CHEJU ISLAND HEDGE MAZE

**BELOW**
*This aerial photograph shows Cheju Island's giant hedge maze when it was newly planted. Surrounded by lush vegetation, it is a truly impressive sight.*

**RIGHT**
*This fence maze at Coconut Creek in Panama City, Florida, is one of America's most established puzzle mazes, covering a complete acre with its two miles of paths.*

This hedge maze on Cheju Island in South Korea was commissioned by the university there. The outline shape of the maze echoes the coastline of the island itself, and a wild pony and the shipwreck of an early European sailing ship that foundered on the island's coast are also portrayed in the lines of hedges. The goal – represented here by an oval at the top of the maze – is actually a giant statue of a man, carved in a style that is characteristic of the island. Enter through the parting waterfall and pass through the gap in the hedges on your right. After solving the maze, visitors cross by high-level bridge to the giant statue, ascend within it, and then leave by way of a final bridge. Directly below the waterfall is a viewing platform, and to the right of that is a cherry picker from which aerial photographs can be taken.

# The Solutions

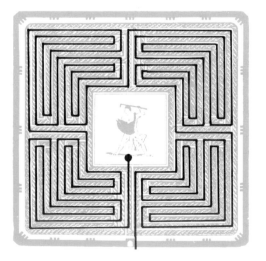

"THESEUS SLAYING THE MINOTAUR"
PAVEMENT MAZE *p.12*

## SOLVING THE MAZES

In this section, you will find the solutions to all the interactive mazes featured in this book. We have shown the shortest routes here, but there are other options. Compare the route you have marked on your acetate sheet with those illustrated here.

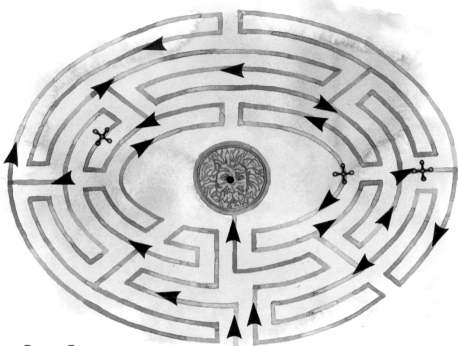

BATH FESTIVAL
MAZE *p.14*

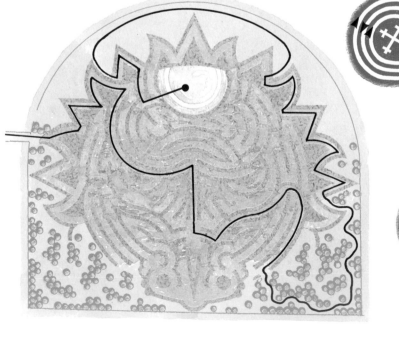

SEVILLE ROMAN MOSAIC MAZE *p.15*

LONGLEAT SUN MAZE *p.16*

ROBIN HOOD'S
RACE *p.21*

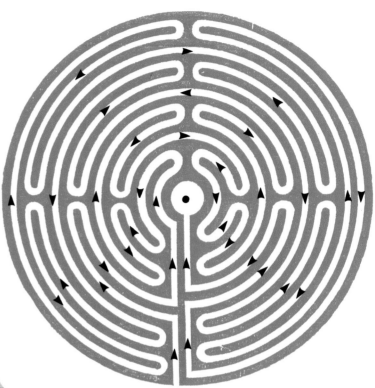

JULIAN'S BOWER *p.22*

VERONICA'S MAZE *p.23*

RIPPON COMMON
TURF MAZE *p.23*

PIMPERNE
TURF MAZE *p.26*

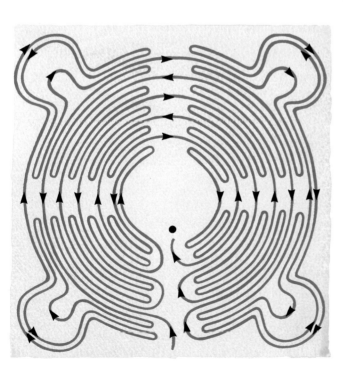

SAFFRON WALDEN TURF MAZE *p.25*

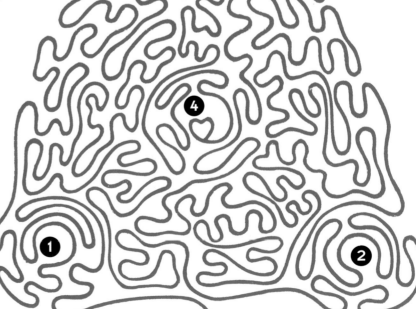

ENGLISH TURF MAZE *p.26*

WINCHESTER MIZMAZE *p.27*

CHARTRES CATHEDRAL PAVEMENT MAZE *p.32*

ST. OMER PAVEMENT MAZE *p.33*

SEGALA'S SHIP *p.35*

ELY CATHEDRAL PAVEMENT MAZE *p.36*

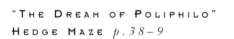

ST. QUENTIN
PAVEMENT MAZE *p.34*

VERSAILLES FABLE MAZE *p.42*

"THE DREAM OF POLIPHILO"
HEDGE MAZE *p.38–9*

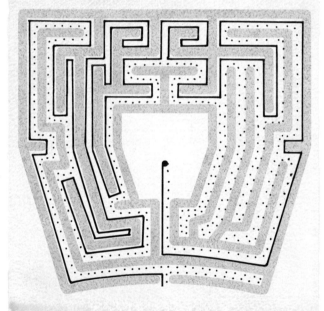

HAMPTON
COURT HEDGE
MAZE *p.48*

left-hand method . . . . . .
right-hand method ———

THREE LANDS
POINT HEDGE
MAZE *p.43*

through 5 fountains ———
through 3 fountains . . . . . . .
to the goal – – – – – – –

WILLIAMSBURG
HEDGE MAZE
*p.49*

left-hand method 28 coins ———
right-hand method 27 coins . . . . .

GLENDURGAN
HEDGE MAZE
*p.51*

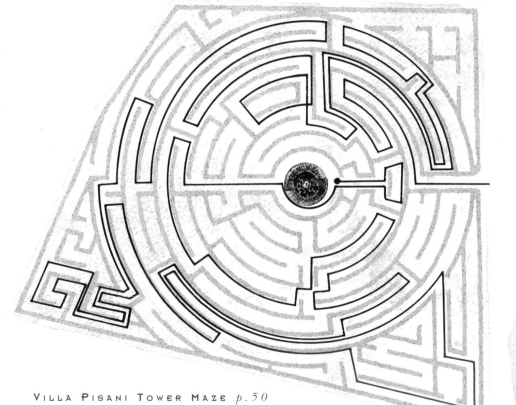

VILLA PISANI TOWER MAZE *p.50*

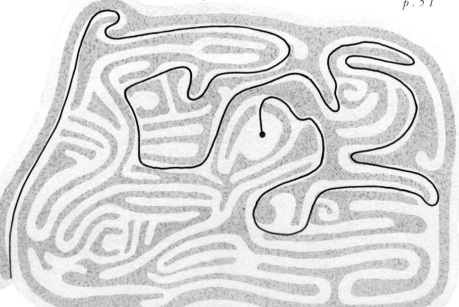

**CHEVENING HEDGE MAZE** *p. 52*

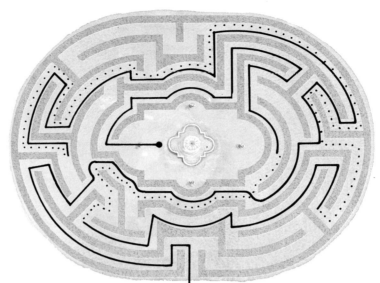

**ITALIANATE MAZE** *p. 53*

flames down; fountains up ————

fountains down; flames up ........

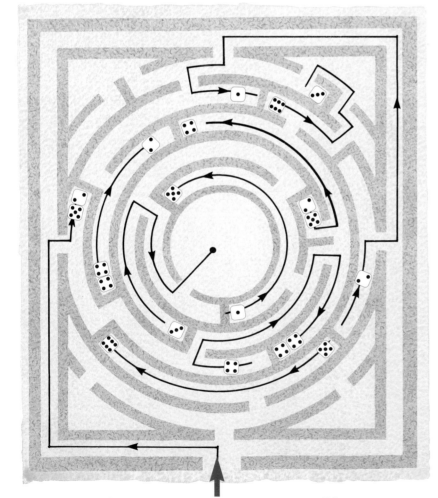

**CHATSWORTH HEDGE MAZE** *p. 55*

**SAFFRON WALDEN HEDGE MAZE** *p. 54*

**RUSSBOROUGH HEDGE MAZE** *p. 56*

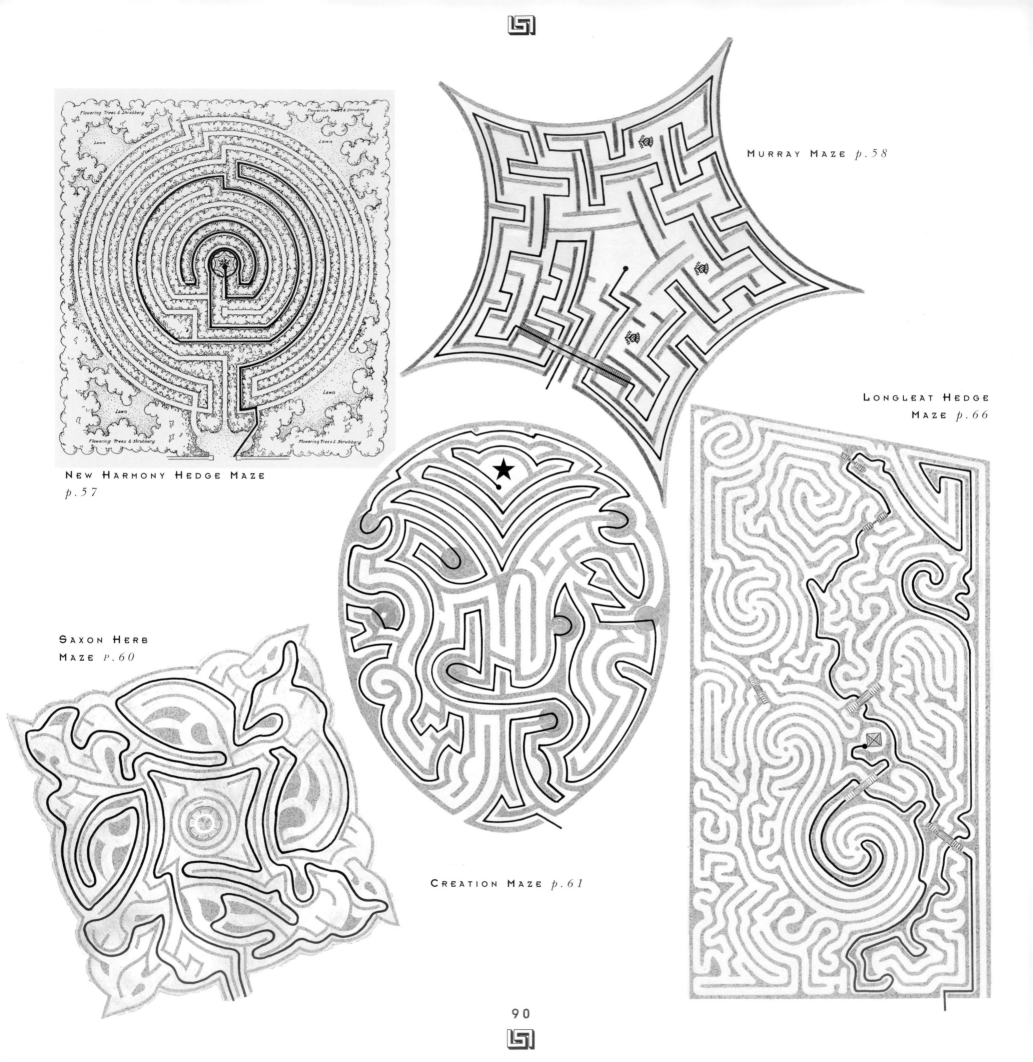

NEW HARMONY HEDGE MAZE
*p.57*

SAXON HERB
MAZE *P.60*

MURRAY MAZE *p.58*

LONGLEAT HEDGE
MAZE *p.66*

CREATION MAZE *p.61*

LEEDS CASTLE
HEDGE MAZE *p.68*

THREE FLAGS COLOR
MAZE *p.70*

DRAGON MIRROR
MAZE *p.71*

TWO GRAY HILLS COLOR MAZE *p.69*

MAZE OF THE
PLANETS *p.72*

carrying no buckets  - - - - -

carrying 1 bucket  ———

carrying 2 buckets  · · · · · · ·

ARCHERY MAZE *p.73*

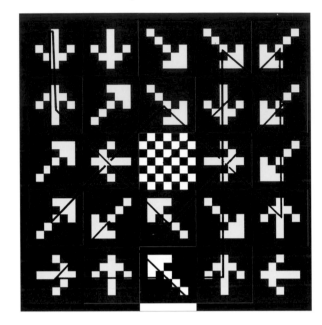

ONE-WAY RAILWAY MAZE *p.76*

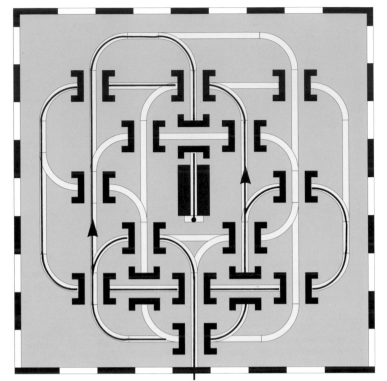

KNIGHT'S MAZE *p.74*

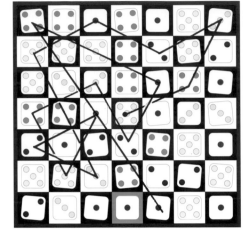

BISHOP'S MAZE *p.74*

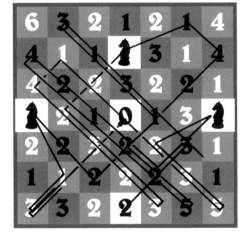

SNOWFLAKE COLOR
MAZE *p.75*

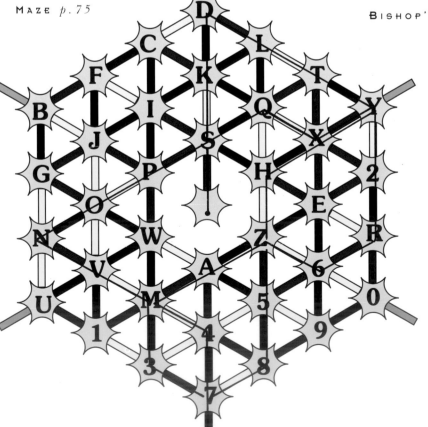

NEW ORLEANS
COLOR MAZE
*p.77*

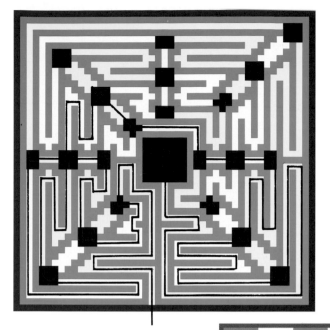

ZIGGURAT COLOR
MAZE *p.78*

GOLDEN HINDE AMAZING
MAIZE MAZE *p.80*

NUMBER MAZE *p.79*

LOCOMOTIVE AMAZING
MAIZE MAZE *p.81*

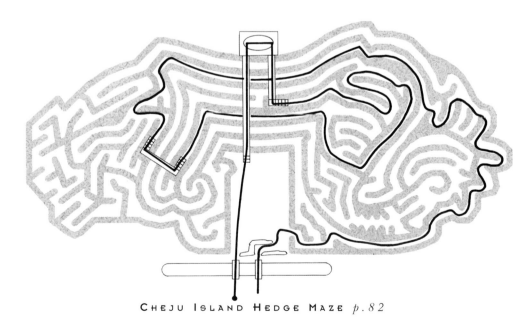

CHEJU ISLAND HEDGE MAZE *p.82*

# CREDITS

**PHOTOGRAPHIC ACKNOWLEDGMENTS**

Quarto would like to thank the following for providing pictures used in this book. While every effort has been made to acknowledge copyright holders, we would like to apologize should there have been any omissions.

Key: a above, b below, r right, l left, c center

AKG: London 18

Ashcombe Maze: 6bl

Moira Clinch: 32bl

Comstock/George Gerster: 2–3, 11, 28–9, 31, 44–5, 62–3

Adrian Fisher: 7ar, 12, 14br, 17br, 20br, 22bl, 23cr, 24b, 25br, 34bl, 36al, 37ar, 47, 48bl, 59ar, 64ar, 66bl, 68bl, 69b, 70br, 71br, 72br, 73ar, 73br, 74bl, 76al, 77br, 78al, 78ar, 80al, 81br, 82bl, 83, front of jacket b, back of jacket a

Fortean Picture Library: 6–7, 10ar, 13bl, 15al, 20al, 21al, 22ar, 23a, 24a, 25bl, 26, 30ar, 32br, 34ar, 41, 50bl, front of jacket ar, cl

Garden Matters: 13ar, 57br

Harry Smith Collection: 33ar, 46br, 51br, 52br, 55ar

Julian Cotton: 59bl

Kentwell Hall Maze: 67ar

Labyrint Drielandenpunt Vaals: 43br

Longleat: 8–9

Howard Loxton: 21ar

Rex Features: 51bl, 67b

Roger-Viollet, Paris: 15br

R. Scott: 60bl

Stjernstrom: 17ar

Visual Arts Library: 1, 15ar, 37b

**ADRIAN FISHER** lives in Portsmouth, England, with Marie and their five children Felicity, Katharine, Julian, Aidan, and Monica. He has created over 135 mazes worldwide, writes and broadcasts prolifically, and travels extensively on both sides of the Atlantic in the course of his work. He can be contacted at:

Adrian Fisher Maze Design
Victoria Lodge, 5 Victoria Grove, Portsmouth PO5 1NE
Telephone: +44 1705 355 500
Fax: +44 1705 350 954
Email: adrian@maze.demon.co.uk

Of the interactive mazes featured in this book, Adrian created all of the extra puzzles that we have added, plus the original designs of the following mazes:

Theseus Slaying the Minotaur Pavement Maze *page 12*
Bath Festival Maze *page 14*
Veronica's Maze *page 23*
Dream of Poliphilo Hedge Maze *pages 38–9*
Three Lands Point Hedge Maze *page 43*
Italianate Maze *page 53*
Russborough Hedge Maze *page 56*
Murray Maze *page 58*
Saxon Herb Maze *page 60*
Leeds Castle Hedge Maze (with Randoll Coate and Vernon Gibberd) *page 68*
Two Grey Hills Color Maze *page 69*
Three Flags Color Maze *page 70*
Dragon Mirror Maze *page 71*
Maze of the Planets *page 72*
Archery Maze *page 73*
Knight's Maze *page 74*
Bishop's Maze *page 74*
Snowflake Color Maze *page 75*
One-way Railway Maze *page 76*
New Orleans Color Maze *page 77*
Ziggurat Colour Maze *page 78*
Number Maze *page 79*
Golden Hinde Amazing Maize Maze *page 80*
Locomotive Amazing Maize Maze *page 81*
Cheju Island Hedge Maze *page 82*

The following mazes pictured in the book were also designed by Adrian Fisher: Nautical Maze (with Gillespies) *page 64*; Tudor Rose Maze *page 67*; Blenheim Palace Maze (with Randoll Coate) *page 67*; Maze of Motor Cars *page 74*; four Abbotswood brick mazes *page 76*; Maze for the Blind *page 78*; Stegosaurus Amazing Maize Maze *page 79*.

Each of the three following one-year temporary mazes created by Adrian Fisher established new world records, both for total area covered and total path length: Stegosaurus Maze, Golden Hinde Maze, and Quadricycle Maze, all in the United States. In 1997, his Windmill Maze at Millet's Farm Center, Oxfordshire, England, surpassed all of these with over 4 miles of paths.

The Pineapple Maze in Hawaii, opening October 1997, is expected to become the world's largest permanent hedge maze, covering an area of 100,000 square feet with 1.7 miles of paths.